LINCOLN BIBLE INSTITUTE

P9-DEO-015

Entrusted with the Gospel

BOOKS BY
DAVID A. MACLENNAN
Published by The Westminster Press

Entrusted with the Gospel
Pastoral Preaching

Entrusted
with
the Gospel

WARRACK LECTURES ON PREACHING

by
David A. MacLennan

Philadelphia
THE WESTMINSTER PRESS

COPYRIGHT, MCMLVI, BY W. L. JENKINS

All rights reserved — no part of this book may be reproduced in any form without permission in writing from the publisher, except by a reviewer who wishes to quote brief passages in connection with a review in magazine or newspaper.

Library of Congress Catalog Card Number: 56–8426

PRINTED IN THE UNITED STATES OF AMERICA

251
M16e
C.1.

Westminster Press

$ 1.20

Oct 31 '56

In proud and loving memory of
my Lowland mother
Effie Mitchell Kellock
and of my Highland father
Alexander Kenneth MacLennan, B.D., D.D.

12222

Contents

7

Foreword

In 1798 the redoubtable Smith of Smiths, Rev. Sydney, lived in Edinburgh while acting as tutor of an English youth. In a characteristically candid letter to his pupil's mother, he wrote his impressions of Scottish life and character. He found the women " handsomer than English women " and " their dialect very agreeable." To him the eighteenth century Scots were " a cautious, and a discreet people . . . very much in earnest in their religion, tho' less so than they were."

If Sydney Smith could have known that Scottish churchmen would invite a North American to lecture on preaching to Scottish theological students and ministers, he might have revised his estimate of Scots' cautiousness and discretion! He would certainly comment caustically on the audacity of such a visitor bringing his homiletical coals to world-famous centers of the mining industry.

In the same letter (*The Letters of Sydney Smith,* edited by Nowell C. Smith, Oxford, the Clarendon Press, 1953, p. 21) the discerning English cleric made two remarks which the changes of one and a half

9

centuries have not rendered inaccurate. Both remarks
make my task more daunting. " In Scotland," he said,
" the clergy are extremely active in the discharge of
their functions, and are from the hold they have on
the minds of the people a very important body of
men." Such diligent and competent men scarcely
need counsel concerning one of their principal functions. As if this were insufficient to discourage a visiting lecturer, he cited the qualities of Scottish lay folk.
" The common people are extremely conversant with
the Scriptures, are really not so much pupils as for-
midable critics to their preachers; many of them are
well read in controversial divinity." Thereupon he
concluded justly, " They are perhaps in some points
of view the most remarkable nation in the world."

Such implied warning notwithstanding, when I was
honored with the invitation to give the Warrack Lectures of 1955, I accepted with alacrity and joy. This
lectureship brings me to " the rock whence I was
hewn." Despite the apostle's warning to shun genealo-
gies, I have been ever grateful that, in what they
would rightly call the providence of God, my ances-
tors on both sides chose Scotland for their birthplace.
One of mother's parents came from the kingdom of
Fife and the other from Covenanters' stock in gray
Galloway. My father's people emigrated earlier from
Rosshire to Nova Scotia, being members of a sturdy
group who enriched the new world far more than
they did the coffers of the landlords who drove them
out. They went out seeking a country far from " the
lone shieling on the misty island," but always they
kept their heart and speech Highland and " in their

dreams beheld the Hebrides." An early memory is of my father crooning a Gaelic lullaby to his bairn in a Canadian manse. In my veins must linger remnants of the Shorter Catechism intermixed with oatmeal and a few lilting phrases from that language which Gaels are sure was spoken in the Garden of Eden!

Had my background been otherwise, I might have yielded to the promptings of reason and humility and gratefully declined the honor offered me. After all, it is a matter of record that my distinguished predecessors in this lectureship have plowed the field intensively and extensively. What comes after may be at best only harrowing — in more than one sense. Nevertheless, it seemed better to fly in the face of wise counsel and factual evidence than to set oneself against what seemed the force of predestination!

To the members of the Church of Scotland Committee on the Education of the Ministry; to my kindly hosts, the Reverend Principal John Mauchline, D.D., of Trinity College, Glasgow, and the Very Reverend Professor G. D. Henderson, D.D., Master of Christ's College, Aberdeen; and to many other friends of whose hospitality my wife and I have been most willing recipients, I give my warmest thanks.

DAVID A. MACLENNAN

Acknowledgments

Grateful acknowledgment is made to the following publishers for permission to quote from their copyrighted publications:

Abingdon Press: *Here I Stand,* by Roland Bainton, 1950.

Ballantine Books, Inc.: a quotation from Richard Eberhart in *New Poems,* edited by Rolfe Humphries, 1953.

Hodder & Stoughton, Ltd.: " Judgment," by G. A. Studdert-Kennedy in the book *The Unutterable Beauty,* by the same author.

Houghton Mifflin Company: the poem " At twenty, stooping round about . . ." by Archibald MacLeish.

Alfred A. Knopf, Inc.: *Of Whales and Men,* by R. B. Robertson.

The Macmillan Company: *Letters to Young Churches,* translated by J. B. Phillips, 1950.

The Gospels, translated by J. B. Phillips, 1953.

The New Yorker: An excerpt from the " Notes and Comment " department, December 12, 1953.

"The Revised H-Bomb Instructions Blues," by Frances Minturn Howard, in the issue of April 10, 1954.

Oxford University Press: *White Collar,* by C. Wright Mills, 1951.

The Firstborn, by Christopher Fry, 1952.

The Boy with a Cart, by Christopher Fry, 1951.

Penguin Books, Inc.: *The Smith of Smiths,* by Hesketh Pearson.

Random House, Inc.: *He Brings Great News,* by Clemence Dane, 1945.

The Viking Press, Inc.: "The Day After Sunday," in *The Love Letters of Phyllis McGinley.* Published originally in *The New Yorker.* Copyright, 1952, by Phyllis McGinley.

"But just as we have been approved by God to be *entrusted with the gospel*, so we speak, not to please men, but to please God who tests our hearts." — *I Thessalonians 2:4.*

"He has entrusted me with the message of his reconciliation." — *II Corinthians 5:19 (Moffatt)*.

"I am entrusted with a commission." — *I Corinthians 9:17.*

"Do not fear to repeat what has already been said. Men need [the truth] dinned into their ears many times from all sides. The first rumor makes them prick up their ears, the second registers, the third enters." — *René Théophile Hyacinthe Laënnec (1781–1826), Regius Professor of Medicine, Collège de France.*

I. *"Entrusted with a Commission"*
— I Corinthians 9:17

Whales and whaling exert a powerful fascination on the minds and imaginations of men. Is this why the Old Testament's greatest missionary tract — The Book of Jonah — is still for many people associated with a whale? Even if Matthew (ch. 12:40) had not so designated the great fish, readers would have identified it as an ancient ancestor of Moby Dick. Too many persons have let the Biblical whale run away with them on voyages less profitable than that given Jonah. It is easier to evade disturbing truth by preoccupation with secondary matters than to confront the fact of God's love for all mankind and his will for us in the light of it.

Here let me insert what medieval homilists called a gloss. When you plan your next sermon on the world-wide mission of the Church, look again at The Book of Jonah. Taking as proposition and recurring theme the response of Peter's erstwhile critics — " to the Gentiles also God has granted repentance unto life " (Acts 11:18) — you could give a brief, relevant, and interesting treatment of the four acts in this drama of the divine missionary imperative. Each chapter furnishes a heading. Somewhere I discovered this outline:

> Act I. Running from God ("But Jonah rose to flee to Tarshish from the presence of the Lord." Jonah 1:3).
>
> Act II. Running to God ("Then Jonah prayed to the Lord his God from the belly of the fish." Ch. 2:1).
>
> Act III. Running with God ("Then the word of the Lord came to Jonah the second time, saying, 'Arise, go to Nineveh, that great city, and proclaim to it the message that I tell you.' So Jonah arose and went to Nineveh." Ch. 3:1, 2).
>
> Act IV. Running Ahead of God ("But it [Nineveh's repentance] displeased Jonah exceedingly, and he was angry." Ch. 4:1).

Within such a framework could be expounded the Christian message that darkness always follows flight from God and his purpose of world redemption; that man's sin is God's sorrow; that true repentance may avert global catastrophe as it does end personal heartbreak; that God, whose love knows not national or racial boundaries, would have us love all men in Christ as he loves them, and give ourselves to the task of winning them. Wrote a contemporary analyst of world conditions: " Human society can be saved only by universalism. [By this term he denoted the divine-human concern for all mankind rather than the theological dogma commonly known by this name.] Unless Christian churches return to this central doctrine of their religion and make it the central doctrine of their practice, they will vanish before the irresistible power of a new religion of universalism " (Emory Reeves, *The Anatomy of Peace*).

But whales and the methods of men who hunt them suggest a leading question concerning Christian preaching in our age. Our Lord spoke of his disciples as fishers of men. Is preaching as a means of taking men for him not outmoded? In his classic allegory of the whale, Herman Melville extolled the pulpit as " earth's foremost part." Would objective appraisal of the pulpit's place in today's world issue in such a high estimate?

A Scottish physician who joined an Antarctic whaling expedition recently related an interesting fact regarding the modern whaling fleet's equipment. On the largest or factory ship the flying bridge presents a combination of the electronic age and that of the ancient mariner. On this bridge is the main radar set, continuously scrutinizing the sea to the horizon and beyond, reporting on the screen every floating object for miles around. Below the radar eye the electronic direction finding apparatus operates. Here also is an old-fashioned magnetic compass, identical with the mariner's compasses of earliest whaling vessels, and not very different from the suspended loadstone of primitive Chinese navigators. Below the bridge in the wheelhouse and chartroom stand duplicate gyro-compasses with dials that read accurately to the thousandth of a minute. Why the obsolete compass when the latest electronic devices for accurate, safe navigation are available and used? The Board of Trade requires that every British ship shall carry a mariner's compass. There on the flying bridge of the huge modern whaler it stands, as it has stood on ships for over six hundred years.

Another museum piece occupies a prominent place. This consists of a wooden rack containing six bright-red iron buckets with plaited-rope handles, the ship's fire-fighting equipment according to standards laid down and never modified by the Board of Trade. Yet below these buckets, which would have been appropriate for use on Drake's galleon, is an electronic warning system, which immediately signals the bridge if any adverse temperature change occurs in any compartment of the ship, together with the latest apparatus for piping foam and other fire-extinguishing chemicals to any place aboard at the press of a button (R. B. Robertson, *Of Whales and Men*).

Mariner's compass and gyrocompasses, fire buckets and electronic fire fighters — does something like this contrast of the antique and the modern confront us when we examine pulpit preaching and modern media of mass communication?

Is the Church a kind of ecclesiastical Board of Trade requiring its officers to retain obsolescent types of communication in an age when audio-visual aids — radio and television broadcasting, motion pictures (cinema) for example — are not only available but preferred by those who should be on the receiving end of the gospel's proclamation?

Not grudgingly but gladly do we concede the ef-

fectiveness of modern instruments of transmitting
the good news of Christ to those who will not expose
themselves to the Word as it is proclaimed in the tra-
ditional service of the Church at worship. Parish ministers who utilize Christian motion pictures, radio,
and television facilities may regret the paucity of the
resources available to them; generally they testify to
their helpfulness. If by any means we may save some,
we shall give God praise for novel, ingenious instruments of preaching, and use them increasingly.

Obviously it is not preaching that is in question.
Preaching in the sense of proclamation proceeds at a
vastly accelerated pace, much of it capable of being baptized into Christ. Under judgment today is
preaching as it has been known since the first prophet
lifted up his voice to declare God's word to those who
would listen; preaching in the tradition of the apostles, reformers, and evangelists of the Christian centuries. Under critical scrutiny is today's preaching of
the truth as it is in Jesus within the context of the
redemptive community of Christ engaged in corporate praise and prayer. More than one has remarked
the audacity of a man standing up in a pulpit to speak
as God's herald to his fellows. Multitudes who give
the local church absent treatment year in and year
out imply that to them preaching is not only auda-
cious and absurd; it is futile. By their indifference,
occasionally disguised in an attitude of patronizing
affability, we know their answer to our question.
More disquieting is another fact. Now and again one
who received authority to preach the Word and administer the sacraments is himself infected by this

low view and openly or covertly disparages this office of the ministry.

You may recall hearing that the first duke of Wellington had a short answer to the young parson who asked his opinion concerning what was then foreign missions. Did his grace not think that in view of crying needs at home the Church should desist from that emphasis? What was the good of unsettling the views of contented heathens with Christianity? To which the old soldier is alleged to have rejoined, "Young man, what are your marching orders? ' Go ye into all the world, and preach the gospel to every creature.'" We have our orders. To us has been given on behalf of Christ to preach the glorious gospel of the blessed God. Nineteen centuries of Christian experience have demonstrated that a chief way of fulfilling this Commission is through the "foolishness of preaching" Christ from the pulpits of our churches week in and week out. Such preaching, God knows, and in our honest hours we know, should be better than it is. Such preaching should be more at the center than on the circumference of the gospel, should be more relevant, clearer, more compelling. But concerning the directive from Him who is our divine commander and friend, there can be no doubt: "Go . . . preach."

In one of the earliest Christian scriptures, Saint Paul put it unforgettably:

> "For our appeal does not spring from error
> or uncleanness, nor is it made with guile; but
> just as we have been approved by God to be
> entrusted with the gospel, so we speak, not to

please men, but to please God who tests our
hearts " (I Thess. 2:3, 4) .

" We speak under the solemn sense of being entrusted with the Gospel," is J. B. Phillips' paraphrase.
You and I to whom by God's amazing grace the Lord
Jesus Christ came as Saviour have been called to his
service. This call may have come in a sudden arrest
and radical change of direction on some Damascus
road. It may have come as quietly as the silent prayer
of a mother or father or friend wings its way to the
Presence. It may have come in a realized sense of human need that we can help to meet or through the
witness of a life thrown away for Christ's sake and for
the sake of others. God's Spirit may have used a wise
counselor to help us to hear and interpret that vocational summons. Softly as dew falls on quiet meadow,
or thunderously in the impact of some shattering
revelation, the call came. But if we were called, and
we know we were, the necessity to preach the gospel
was laid upon us. That which we do in the pulpit, as
in every place to which the service of Christ leads us,
must be, as Paul wrote to Timothy (I Tim. 1:11)
" in accordance with the glorious gospel of the blessed
God with which I have been entrusted."

Not once or twice but again and again, confirma-
tion of this call is given the faithful and receptive
preacher, becoming a conviction of the mind and a
pulse in the blood. Then it is that sermon making
and sermon delivery become an exhilaration and a
price one would gladly pay for the privilege of doing.
But for most of us — particularly those of us who

may be plagued by a Celtic demon! — there come
the hours of murky gray, when the splendor seems
to have faded and no vein of fire courses through our
deflated spirits. In such dark hours it is immensely
steadying to remember that we have been entrusted
with the gospel, and entrusted with the task of its
proclamation. Then we too can say, " I thank him
who has given me strength for this, Christ Jesus our
Lord, because he judged me faithful by appointing
me to his service." Yes, in spite of the failures and
sinning, he judged us worthy to speak in his name.
" Foremost of sinners " may be the humiliating truth
about ourselves that we must confess, but such acknowledgment is but prelude to our acceptance by
Him, and our self-acceptance in him. " Foremost of
sinners; but I received mercy for this reason, that in
me, as the foremost, Jesus Christ might display his
perfect patience for an example to those who were
to believe in him for eternal life " (I Tim. 1:15, 16) .

Is the pulpit an anachronism? Is Christian preaching from the pulpits of our churches not only discredited by the vast majority of our nominally Protestant fellow citizens but a second-best means of
proclaiming the Word of God? Doubtless the power
of a long and once-hallowed tradition will keep us at
it, as the bosun on a modern ship regularly fills the fire
buckets because he knows it is required and not because he believes the ship's welfare depends on it.
Cynics may say that we will continue to go through
our Sunday stint, not because we have a high view
of its significance, but because it represents a vested
interest; to discard the practice would threaten our

status and security. But when did an honest man, let alone a Christian one, persist in a performance that he knew to be largely devoid of meaning and power? And when did a conscript of Christ permit a cynic to intimidate him, or the counsels of discouragement to deflect him from what he was persuaded was God's will for His Church and for his ministers? " We have been approved by God to be entrusted with the Gospel, so we speak." Here, then, is the reason for hurling a ringing " No! " at our question, Is the pulpit and its preaching obsolete? God, the eternal Creator and Redeemer and Lord of all life, has made himself known to men supremely in the life and death and resurrection of the Lord Jesus Christ. In the mysterious action of the Holy Spirit this divine Redeemer and Lord confronted us in his holy love. Our response of loving trust and obedience was his gift also, and by that response he has saved and is saving us to newness of life. Within and to the fellowship of his body, the Church, he called us to be his representatives and messengers: " The church, of which I became a minister according to the divine office which was given to me for you, to make the word of God fully known " (Col. 1:24, 25). " For I am a minister of the Church by Divine commission, a commission granted to me for your benefit and for a special purpose: that I might fully declare God's Word — that sacred mystery " (J. B. Phillips, *Letters to Young Churches*). To us, despite our unworthiness and ineptness, he gave the Commission to preach his word of judgment and of mercy, of wisdom and of power. " For this I was appointed a preacher " (I Tim. 2:7). While we

do not regard any mode of preaching his Word as
sacrosanct or incapable of change, the experience of
the Church throughout its existence convinces us that
the preaching of the Word to men and women as-
sembled in his house for communion with him is a
singularly effectual means of grace which he has or-
dained. " Since we have the same spirit of faith as he
had who wrote, ' I believed, and so I spoke,' we too
believe, and so we speak " (II Cor. 4:13) .

A Russian writer — was it Turgenev? — once
stoutly asserted that if, as seemed to him incredible,
the savants of the world proved conclusively that
Christ was utterly wrong in his interpretation of
reality and his religion no revelation but a great illusion, he would take his stand with the discredited
Galilean. He preferred, he said, to be wrong with
Christ than right with any other. It was a gallant but
unnecessary avowal of love. No such alternative will
ever face the believer. Our tremendous faith is self-
authenticating. " Why are you so sure of heaven? "
asked a heckler of a Salvation Army preacher. " Because I have been there, by God's grace," quietly
answered the simple witness. We too have " been
there," have had of his reality and love rich and in-
controvertible evidence. " Our appeal does not spring
from error or uncleanness, nor is it made with guile;
but just as we have been approved by God to be entrusted with the gospel, so we speak, not to please
men, but to please God who tests our hearts."

What will this conviction concerning our preaching ministry do for us?

First, *it will gain or recover for us a true perspec-*

tive on our task. If the gospel is viewed in New Testament terms as an entrustment, then its proclamation to men must be a " top priority " in our ministry. This does not mean that the preparation and delivery of sermons should be an exclusive preoccupation of the minister. To every man " in orders " and under orders is given the gift of ministry. This gift is varied in its character and wide in its scope. We are to preach the Word and also administer the sacraments, " bear rule " in the congregation, engage in all that is meant by the cure of souls, do the work of a Christian educator, and all the rest. The most ardent advocate of preaching must not emulate the harassed client who, when asked by his lawyer how much he should claim for him in the court trial then proceeding, telegraphed, " Claim everything! " It is possible to claim too much, and thereby weaken our case. There have been times and places in which the Christian cause has suffered because its official representatives have concentrated on one office or function of the ministry to the neglect of all others. Lay folk have justifiably assumed that the minister had no need of them, was not genuinely concerned with their toil and trouble, when their only sight and sound of him was in the pulpit on the Lord's Day, with an occasional fleeting glimpse of the man of God on his daily flight from manse to post office and back again. Such Olympian aloofness convinced not a few laymen that they had no need of the parson. One of the hardiest fallacies circulated among us is that, notwithstanding our educational advantages, personal equipment, and the time at our disposal, we cannot be both

pastors and preachers. On the contrary, a strong case
can be made for the contention that a man who does
not exercise faithfully and lovingly his pastoral ministry cannot preach for long to the condition of his
people. Certainly, with the possible exception of the
jet-propelled " big name preacher " (as Americans
sometimes describe the popular orator occupying the
large city pulpit), the common people will not hear
him gladly — if they hear him at all.

Nor is it otherwise with the minister who, in order to devote all his time to sermon making, skimps
on the preparation of his part in the conduct of public worship. " You spoke, Doctor, as if you had come
straight from the courts of the King," said a parish-
ioner to Alexander Whyte after a service. " And perhaps I did," said the old saint. One does not con-
sciously seek to give this impression; no man may
come from the Mount where he has kept rendezvous
with the Lord knowing that his spirit shines. By the
same token, no man may ascend the pulpit and be
sure that he is qualified to dispense the sacrament of
the Word who has not first and last prepared himself,
his prayers, the Scripture reading, and every other
act of worship as painstakingly and Christianly as he
has prepared his sermon. Learned and devout men of
the Church of Scotland have contributed greatly to
our understanding of our heritage of Christian worship. They have reminded us that every adequate
service should unite the essential elements of the
synagogue service and that of the upper room. Rich
liturgical resources have been placed at our disposal
in recent years, which should be known and discern-

ingly used by every minister. But in every Protestant something of the prejudice or soundness of Jenny Geddes toward prayer books lingers! Of course, read prayers need never short-circuit the divine current as it moves to light lamps of faith and love. Who would deny that the noble petitions and majestic diction of a *Book of Common Prayer* may be infinitely more edifying than the graceless hodgepodge of unpremeditated " free prayer "? I find no warrant in Scripture for believing that the Holy Spirit favors rambling, awkward, and tediously long prayers simply because the man who offers them is pious and sincere. But does not much depend on how we read them and what we read? Whether we read from the great prayers of the Church or not, must we not also offer confessions, thanksgivings, intercessions, which come from our own intimate awareness of our people's needs and of God's gracious provision for them? Can we do this if we defer our own preparation of the service to those frequently hectic moments just before we enter the house of God?

If we see our ministry of preaching as an entrustment, the various aspects of the total task committed to us take their rightful places. It will not be worship *or* preaching, pastoral counseling *or* pulpit work, Christian social service *or* the exposition of God's Word; it will be, as it always has been for the perceptive minister, " both . . . and." Nevertheless, because we accept the Biblical view of preaching and unrepentantly stand in the tradition of the Reformation, we shall give primary place to sermon making. As to the kind of sermons we should strive to make,

much has been said by my gifted predecessors as well
as by many other wise teachers. More will be said in
the present series.

A second consequence of accepting the New Testament view of preaching should prove reassuring to
the novice as to the veteran in the ministry: *we shall
be delivered from taking our task either too lightly
or too seriously*. I am not sure which attitude is worse,
or more prevalent among us. To take our preaching
too lightly may mean that almost anything will do
for a sermon, provided there is at least a Biblical reference, one or two " good illustrations," and that we
can deliver it with reasonable freedom in that unctu-
ous tone which Mark Twain described somewhat ir-
reverently as " the Heavenly Father voice "!

Taking preaching lightly may mean following a
line that ultimately may prove morally and spiritually more disastrous to hearers and preachers alike
than casual, slovenly treatment of the message. We
give our hearers what they want instead of what,
through brooding on God's Word and their true condition, we know they need.

> There was a clergyman out in Dumont
> Who kept tropical fish in his font,
>   Although it surprises
>   The babes he baptizes
> It seems to be just what they want.

More than the apocryphal minister of Dumont give
people what they want. It is not underestimating
their intelligence or spiritual maturity to say that
many want a diet of breezy, banal capsules of self-

help, usually deficient in spiritual vitamins. Sermons of this quality manifestly lack a dimension of depth because they resemble only distantly the gospel of Christ. Verily such purveyors to the people's taste have their reward. On our side of the Atlantic the reward in prestige and emoluments is likely to be considerable. But such men, undoubtedly helpful on a superficial level, lay themselves open to the prophet's charge of healing the wound of God's people lightly (Jer. 6:14). To excoriate such accomplished players on a wind instrument (Ezek. 33:32) is not to decry popular preaching. Christian preachers have a duty to be popular in the sense of winning for their Lord the maximum hearing possible. It does not follow that, because there were few around the cross when the Saviour of the world preached his last and greatest sermon, when few come to hear us, we are remotely in his class. Yet I have heard that rationalization offered by a minister who sought to justify his own small congregations. In his case, other factors — notably the population movement away from his parish, plus his own neglect of the gift that was his — operated to produce the discouraging situation he lamented. Nevertheless, to take seriously the preaching of the whole counsel of God may well mean that we shall be denied popularity of the specious, meretricious kind. Like prosperity, popularity can cost too much. " We are not," stoutly asserts the apostle, " fraudulent hucksters of God's message, no peddlers of adulterated goods " (cf. II Cor. 2:17).

When a man realizes that he has been entrusted with a grave responsibility, he cannot act as if it did

not matter how he discharged it. Always he feels the
spur of another's trust and confidence. To remember
that another depends on him, has placed his confidence in him, helps to keep a man responsible and
true to his trust. It is said that in despondent moods
Martin Luther would answer the devil who assailed
him and rally the hero in his soul by saying, " I am
baptized." Recollection of God's unmerited grace in
receiving him into the household of Christ nerved
him afresh to do valiantly for Him whose name he
bore. *We* have been baptized. We are loved creatures.
We have been and are being saved by His abundant
grace. He believes in us, sure that his confidence in
our capability to be faithful stewards of his gospel is
not misplaced. Therefore, we must give our best in
time and toil, in study and imagination, to fulfill our
high calling. There is a vivid and relevant word of
God to the preacher in that strange transaction between David and Ornan the Jebusite, told in both
II Sam., ch. 24 and in I Chron. 21:1–27. Its theology
disturbs us a little; we cannot conceive of the God
and Father of our Lord Jesus Christ destroying seventy thousand men because in a burst of foolish pride
their leader took a national census. Yet through the
earthen vessel gleams a golden insight. Manfully
David acknowledged his responsibility for the num-
bering of the people, repented of whatever his sin
may have been, and asked that he be punished instead of the human sheep who merely obeyed his
orders. The penance prescribed consisted of rearing
an altar to the Lord on a specified farmer's threshing
floor. When David informed the farmer of his pur-

pose, the farmer acted as any loyal subject of the reigning monarch would act. What if it did mean yielding a precious bit of his property and upsetting the harvest operation? " Take it," said Ornan graciously, " and all the animals, wheat, and wood you need. I give it all." " But King David said to Ornan, ' No, but I will buy it for the full price; I will not take for the Lord what is yours, nor offer burnt offerings which cost me nothing.' So David paid." (I cannot resist reminding you that there is a passage which asks to be preached when the theme of stewardship is indicated.) When a lively sense of our trusteeship, our privilege and obligation, affects us, we too will not offer to the Lord that which costs us nothing — or nothing more than the time it takes hastily to jot down notes from a first-aid manual for indolent preachers, adding a few ill-digested ideas simmering on the surface of our minds.

In the early years of this century my mother's father was the minister of three country parishes in eastern Quebec. He never occupied a so-called " great pulpit," but he made those rural pulpits great for more than one farmer and his wife. As a lad visiting him, I overheard him say to a member of his flock at the close of their conversation, in the idiom once familiar to Scottish Presbyterians, " Aye, aye, Donald, and now I must be away to the study to beat some oil for the sanctuary lamps." It is a quaint, dated figure of speech, but it reminded Donald and me that a good minister of Christ took his sermon work seriously. Rev. David Kellock knew that he had been " entrusted with the gospel," and that such entrustment involved conscientious craftsmanship.

To view preaching as an essential part of the task
entrusted to us by our Lord relieves us of much of the
unnecessarily heavy burden too commonly carried by
faithful preachers. Shortly before World War II began, one of England's deservedly famous preachers
confided that, while he loved preaching, the process
of making a sermon was one that literally nauseated
him. He said in effect that he knew the cause was psychosomatic; his agitated mind and fiercely distraught
emotions played havoc with his digestive tract! No
one who knew him and no one who heard him would
ever say that he did not take preaching seriously. He
took it too seriously. He acted as if the Lord de-
pended exclusively on him, and was otherwise engaged during the hours when His servant sweated it
out at his desk. Truly, any worth-while achievement
" takes it out of us." Have you not known in your
own experience, as you strove to help a man or
woman through a deep valley, the truth of our Lord's
saying that he knew that power had gone forth from
him (Luke 8:46), that virtue went out of him? Nevertheless, it is a kind of atheism when we act as if we
were alone, unaided, and wholly inadequate to the
task He has assigned. If he entrusted you with this
" impossible possibility " — of speaking his Word to
your people, so that they will meet and hear him with
a minimum of interference by you — has he not some
responsibility to see you through and see the Word
home? He did not promise that we should find the
going easy in this or in any other venture of discipleship. He pointed to roadblocks on the highway and

said that the road might wind uphill all the way. But he did promise that his grace would be sufficient. So with our actual preaching. Because of temperament and its physical components, tension may be ours to live with until the whistle blows and we homeward run, but chronic and severe tension is unnecessary and may be actually sub-Christian. Can we not do our best in the study, keep ourselves reasonably free from fatigue, then commit ourselves and our poor best to him whose spokesmen we are, and ask him to do the rest? Nothing so delivers a man from self-consciousness in public speaking and dissolves the unworthy fears that make us tense in the pulpit as to realize that " the Word is on us to deliver," that it comes from Another, and that the Other is the great and gracious God who draws near to us in the living, invisible, and invincible Christ. Share the responsibility with him — he loves the burden, and he loves you and your people. " For our appeal," and the act of making it, " does not spring from error," including the error that it is our word that we speak; nor does it spring from " uncleanness " (have we not been made clean even from the stain of our self-love through the word of Christ dwelling in us richly with all wisdom?) ; " nor is it made with guile " (we have no bag of tricks to deceive and impress our hearers) ; " but just as we have been approved by God to be entrusted with the gospel, so we speak, not to please men " — so we need not fear what they may think, or trim our message to win their approval — " but to please God who tests our hearts," and steadies and upholds them too.

II. "*He Brings Great News*"

In December, 1953, employees of New York City's newspapers went on strike. Deprived of their favorite daily reading, residents of "Bagdad-on-the-Subway" made interesting discoveries. Thanks to modern means of communication, they found it possible to learn what was going on in the world from other sources than the daily press. Previously unrealized, also, was the fact that important events could be reported briefly. Even in a verbose age broadcast news bulletins are laconic. A third discovery impressed an editor of the magazine *The New Yorker*. Reflecting on the experience he wrote, " Surely ninety per cent of all so-called news is old stuff — some of it two and three thousand years old " (issue of December 12, 1953) .

He was right. Not only " so-called news " but momentous news concerning fundamental reality and man's nature and destiny is " old stuff — some of it two and three thousand years old." The most significant news ever broadcast to men is as ancient as the eighth century before Christ, as old as the birth date of a Jewish girl's baby boy and the " dream born in a herdsman's shed and written in the secret scriptures of the poor." As men reckon time, the event which Christians designate by the phrase " the Lord Jesus Christ " took place in a corner of a now vanished empire long ago. Biblical authority supports the claim that the event originated before the foundation of the world.

Unlike records of " old, unhappy, far-off things and battles long ago," this divine event of God's self-disclosure and action is *news* — exciting, relevant, and decisive. Not only, as one historian said, because all real history is contemporary history, but because the event reported is forever timely. As we have been reminded, the gospel is timely bcause it is a message telling of the effects of what has happened upon what is now happening. For the Christian message is news from eternity, and eternity keeps no clocks or calendars. To God a thousand years is as one day and one day as a thousand years (II Peter 3:8). The New Testament has a word for it: *kairos*, as distinguished from *chronos*; God's time, transcending chronological time. Let a man receive and believe this glorious good news of God's action in Christ, and he is confronted by One who is his immediate deliverer from his deadliest enemies. The Ancient of Days becomes his present helper. The historic Jesus becomes the eternal contemporary. Moreover, the divine society inaugurated by One who proclaimed and embodied it in his person nineteen hundred years ago is now and here. As Jesus himself said, the Kingdom of God is available, is within your reach. (Professor Henry S. Cadbury, of Harvard University, has pointed out that this is perhaps the most accurate translation of the saying in Luke 17:21 generally rendered " the kingdom of God is within you " (K.J.V.), or, " in the midst of you " (R.S.V.). Any man may enjoy citizenship in this redemptive community, live by its inexhaustible resources, experience its enduring joy and peace — *now*. That which the Church exists to proclaim and demonstrate is as old as God's focused disclosure of himself in the personality of Jesus of Nazareth, and that revelation, asserts the New Testament, was destined before the foundation of the world (I Peter 1:20). It is as old as the record of this revelation in the Christian Scriptures. It is as new as today's sunrise and more necessary to man's true life.

Hence it is *good* news, " the glorious gospel of the blessed God " (I Tim. 1:11). Good news is news of an event that changes the context and alters the sequence of events for the good. And the gospel is the good news of God's doings in the world, which fulfill men's hopes and end the threats to these hopes. Outsiders might not suspect it from the way it is often proclaimed. Weather reports are made with more animation (particularly in Britain when the announcer can promise " bright intervals "!) and clarity than that of many transmitters who announce the astounding news that nineteen hundred years ago something happened to change the moral and spiritual climate of the world; that the Author of life and Lord of history has personally invaded this planet, and that the least of mortals may make contact with him and share in his triumph. Has familiarity with this world-changing event bred listlessness in declaring it? Ten years ago the novelist Clemence Dane published a fictionized account of how the news of the battle of Trafalgar reached Britain. When Admiral Lord Collingwood chose a young naval lieutenant to act as courier, the young man, Lapenotiere, was elated; this was the greatest honor that could be conferred on him. In his little ship he raced to Falmouth, then by horse sped overland to London. In each town through which he passed the citizens who heard his report were exhilarated and saddened: exhilarated because he brought word of Britain's greatest victory, saddened because they learned that the victory cost the life of their hero, Lord Nelson. But all — courier, king, and commoners alike — sensed the epoch-marking significance of his tidings.

> " Give him tending;
> He brings great news "
> (Clemence Dane, *He Brings Great News*) .

The humblest minister of Christ standing in the pulpit of the most obscure church brings great news. Is there greater news than this with which we have been entrusted by our divine Commander — that God has come out victor over the enemies of his Kingdom, has broken the power of sin and death and put to rout the anarchs of the night? Aye, the victory cost our King's life, but God raised him from the dead, of which we are witnesses (cf. Acts 2:32; 3:15; etc.) . Who would not thrill to be commissioned by him to tell the world this great good news? Who would not endure any privation and undertake any discipline

to assure anxious and despairing hearts that the
long, tragic war was victoriously ended, even though
" mopping up " operations must proceed while time
runs on?

> " Sing, O heavens, for the Lord has done it;
>   shout, O depths of the earth;
> break forth into singing, O mountains,
>   O forest, and every tree in it!
> For the Lord has redeemed Jacob,
>   and will be glorified in Israel "
>   (Isa. 44:23) .

Recently in America a one-act play was introduced
on television by one who asked: " When have you
seen a happy headline? Storm, disaster, atomic explo-
sions, accidents, war — these are the headlines we
commonly see. Tonight we shall tell you about a
happy headline." Then followed a pleasant little play
depicting a happy issue out of a family's afflictions.
Christians accept the necessity of reading grim headlines day by day. But they know that the demonic,
the bestial, the apparently meaningless tragedies of
the human situation are not the last word on life
and death. They have read something better than a
" happy headline "; with the eyes of faith they see
beyond the dark " atheistic facts " of heartbreak and
wrecked hopes One who is the first and last word on
everything. They are persuaded that neither death
nor life nor anything else in all creation can separate
them from his love, which they have so richly experienced in Jesus Christ. They know that on the loom

of life, with infinite patience and skill, holy and
righteous Love weaves the warp of evil with the weft
of good into his perfect design. From within the context of the faith, without pious sentimentality, they
can sing,

> " With mercy and with judgment
>   My web of time He wove,
>   And aye the dews of sorrow
>   Were lustered by His love "
> (Anne Ross Cousin, 1824–1906).

It was a realist who declared, " I consider that the
sufferings of this present time are not worth compar-
ing with the glory that is to be revealed to [in] us "
(Rom. 8:18). Why was the apostle so deeply convinced? Because to him and within his deepest self
had been revealed the glory and the glorious purpose of God in the risen Christ. " He who . . . had
called me through his grace, was pleased to reveal his
Son to [in] me " (Gal. 1:15, 16). He had done more
than read the " happy headline "; he had firsthand
knowledge of its truth. " God was in Christ reconciling the world to himself, not counting their tres-
passes against them, and entrusting to us the message
of reconciliation " (II Cor. 5:19). This tremendous
assertion was not fabricated by any reporter nor
dreamed up by any editor. " I would have you know,
brethren, that the gospel which was preached by me
is not man's gospel. For I did not receive it from
man, nor was I taught it, but it came through a revelation of Jesus Christ" (Gal. 1:11, 12).

Having received the gospel and the Commission

to preach it, can we not recapture some of " the first
fine careless rapture " with which it first broke upon
a disillusioned world? Applied to preachers, Browning's adjective " careless " may not be appropriate;
despite the opinion of irreverent youngsters, we are
not birds pouring forth " profuse strains of unpremeditated art." Yet " careless " in this context sug-
gests glad abandon, exultant joy in the privilege of
speaking the lyrical truth as it is in Jesus. Do we
usually give such an impression in our witness? Sir
William Robertson Nicoll, first editor of the *British
Weekly* and an avid hearer of sermons, wrote to a
friend, " It is not often that one hears a sermon obviously spoken with gladness." And an earlier observer
and practicer of the art, Sydney Smith, asked: " Why
are we natural everywhere but in the pulpit? No man
expresses warm and animated feelings anywhere else
with his mouth alone, but with his whole body; he
articulates with every limb, and talks from head to
foot with a thousand voices. Why this holoplexia on
sacred occasions only? Why call in the aid of paralysis
to piety? Is it a rule of oratory to balance the style
against the subject, and to handle the most sublime
truths in the dullest language and the driest manner? Is sin to be taken from men, as Eve was from
Adam, by casting them into a deep slumber? "
(quoted by Hesketh Pearson, in *The Smith of Smiths*,
p. 36, Penguin Books, edition 1948; in association
with Hamish Hamilton) .

Doubtless it would be absurd to suggest that every
preacher should attempt to reproduce the style and
manner implicitly desired by Sydney Smith. He him-

self wrote scathingly of the popular pulpit orator whom he uncharitably lampooned as a " semideliri- ous sectary, who pours forth his animated nonsense with the genuine look and voice of passion." Never- theless we may give the impression that the gospel is a sentence of death instead of life — that it is mainly a demand to practice a repellently austere morality — when we prepare sermons as a kind of penance for venial sins, and then deliver them as if we were " holy lumps of ice, numbed into quiescence and stagnation and mumbling."

Does the seriousness of man's plight, " having no hope and without God in the world " preclude this kind of joyous proclamation? As we fare forth to en- gage doubt, indifference, and the other adversaries lurking to ambush men's souls, is gay knightliness incompatible with our vocation as Christ's ministers? True, " we speak under the solemn sense of being entrusted by God with the Gospel " (I Thess. 2:4, Phillips). It *is* a solemn responsibility, so grave that unless the herald was upheld by Him whom he pre- sents he could not long sustain it. Nevertheless, recog- nition of its seriousness cannot mean that we are to behave in the pulpit or in any other place as if we were mourners at a cosmic wake. " These things I have spoken to you," said the Lord on the eve of his agony and death, " that my joy may be in you, and that your joy may be full " (John 15:11). " These things " included his assurance (1) of our inward cleansing by his word; (2) of our spiritual union with him as intimate as the branches of a vine with the tree; (3) of the fruitfulness of our discipleship;

and (4) of the Father's abiding love. He has spoken these creative words. Despite our fickleness and folly, he has bestowed on us his joy. He admits us to his undying friendship. Can we not speak for him with something of his own grace?

In his short biography of Dr. John Donne, Izaak Walton describes the weekly work schedule assiduously followed by the eminent seventeenth century divine. Respite from what his biographer called " the weary burthen of his week's meditations " and sermon making came on Saturday. Wrote Walton, Donne " usually spent that day in visitation of friends, or some other diversions of his thoughts; and would say that he gave both his body and mind that refreshment, that he might be ' enabled to do the work of the day following, not faintly, but with courage and cheerfulness.' " Twentieth century parish ministers cannot emulate the seventeenth century dean of St. Paul's if they would. Other loads besides " the weary burthen " of the week's meditations must be carried. But we too may so order our days and our souls to do the work of every Lord's Day " not faintly, but with courage and cheerfulness."

We bring great news. Our Lord expects us to tell it greatly.

Does the foregoing plea to preach the gospel in a spirit and manner consonant with its nature imply that the method of preaching is more significant than the content of it? Unequivocally no! Unfortunately, even among ministers, credence is given the unflattering fallacy that it is not what we say but how we say it that matters. In cricket the bowler, in baseball the pitcher, may find delivery of the ball his paramount concern. To mastery of the method such players wisely devote hours of practice. Laymen have been heard inordinately praising a preacher's attractive delivery. In this they find the secret of his " success." But the preacher, no less than the bowler or baseball pitcher, must have something to deliver. To use an American colloquialism, he must have " something on the ball." Also, he must have something *in* it if he is to deliver it. We are not called to release toy balloons but to direct a living Word to a living target. No baseball can be approved for official use unless it has a solid core of specified material. Preaching the good news is infinitely more than a game, and no man may play at it with impunity. That which is entrusted to us to deliver has a solid core. In recent years Biblical theologians beginning with Dr. C. H. Dodd have reminded us of this core, this kerygma, in the apostolic preaching. It consists of the themes preached by the first Christian messengers, and represents the outline of the Early Church's message.

Recall its main elements:

> The promises made in the Old Testament are fulfilled.
>
> The Messiah has come.
>
> He is Jesus of Nazareth, who
>
>> Went about doing good and executing mighty works by the power of God.
>>
>> Was crucified according to the purpose of God.
>>
>> Was raised by God from the dead.

> Is exalted by God and given the name
> above every name.
> Will come again for the judgment and
> restoration of all things.
> Therefore all you who hear the message re-
> pent and be baptized."

What does this core of the Early Church's message
say to us? To some it says little more than relics uncovered by archaeologists say to hurrying tourists taking a quick look at a museum collection. To others
the Scriptural statement expresses hopelessly out-
dated thought-forms of naïve first and second century Christians, concepts entangled with an obsolete
cosmology urgently needing to be " demythologized."
Yet to the Christian whose saving encounter with the
living God is mediated by Biblical revelation, the
affirmations of the early preaching provide an epi-
tome of the gospel. However he may explicate it and
translate it into terms twentieth century man can
grasp, he is sure that these dogmas are indeed gospel
truth, packed for transportation and communication.

Thus, to the needs of our people in this volcanic
era we bring, not tidy formulas or neatly packaged
answers to every imaginable question; we bring the
Word which gives newness of life, and therefore light
and power to find the answers. Without discarding
the permanent contributions of what is called " liberal Christianity," we have something better because
something closer to the gospel's vital center. That
which is committed to us deals more radically with
our human situation and what God has done to meet
it. Years ago as an undergraduate I attended lectures

given by Emil Brunner during one of his first visits
to America. To a large and curious audience he expounded vigorously and unambiguously the classic
Christian position as he understood it. His acceptance
of the tested results of scientific criticism applied to
the Scriptures was apparent. This puzzled some of
his hearers, as they had assumed that the use of the
historical and scientific method in religion reduced
the gospel to the Sermon on the Mount and the
Lord's Prayer, and made the Church's chief task the
promotion of an innocuously untheological type of
religious education. Yet here was a reputable scholar
whose doctrinal position was dynamic orthodoxy.
Brunner's evangelical credo seemed distressingly old-
fashioned. As we left the hall, I overheard two
ministers of a " liberal " Protestant denomination dis-
cussing the man and his thesis. Said one of them wist-
fully, " If I could only accept his premises, I would
have a great gospel to preach — with authority."
Without conceding that Brunner's interpretation or
that of any other Christian thinker may be completely adequate, is it not true that the main points
of the New Testament faith give us a great gospel to
preach? And that when we preach this gospel we are
invested with the authority of God himself? " Our
faith is like that mentioned in the Scripture: I believed and therefore did I speak? For we too speak
because we believe, and we know for certain that He
Who raised the Lord Jesus from death shall also by
Him raise us " (II Cor. 4:13, 14, Phillips) .

What is the gospel to which the apostolic preaching points? It is the good news that the God who re-

veals and gives himself in Jesus Christ is the God who rules and redeems the world by the inexhaustible power of his love.

God so loves that he gives himself to men, and to the world he created and sustains, in order that he may be in fellowship with men and men with him. Nothing in the universe or in human need is beyond the reach of this Love. For he so loved that, like the prodigal's father in Jesus' best-loved story, he ran out to find the seeker after him. He came into human life himself. " God so loved the world that he gave his only Son " (John 3:16) . " God was in Christ personally reconciling the world to Himself " (II Cor. 5:19, Phillips) .

In 1952 the International Missionary Council asked twenty scholars to restate the universal missionary obligation as grounded in the eternal gospel and in relation to the present historical situation. In their report one sentence concerning the gospel strikingly set forth its heart and could provide a fourfold outline for a sermon on basic Christianity: " In Jesus of Nazareth, God is with men — the light of their darkness, the One who alone forgives their sins, the Companion of their loneliness, the Bearer of new and fulfilling possibilities and power for personal and social life." As reporters broadcasting from the front line, standing at the boundary where the old age fights the new age, this is the good tidings that we bring.

To the question, What is the gospel?, the Church makes answer in its historic creeds and in the statements of faith formulated by communions of the

great Church in recent times. Today's preacher does
well to use the Apostles' Creed as a basis for a series
of sermons on the Christian manifesto. Always, however, the preacher, like other Christian individuals,
will " theologize " in terms of his own experience
as this is illumined, corrected, and enlarged by the
experience of the total Christian community. He will
not only tell what God has meant to those of the
past who " looked unto him, and were lightened "
(Ps. 34:5, K.J.V.) , but he will speak from " firsthand
acquaintance with Deity," testifying, " I know whom
I have believed." Paul speaks of " my gospel." There
is a sense in which today's preacher likewise must
fashion his personal version of the unchanging gospel. Providentially " the faith . . . once for all delivered to the saints " was not once for all poured
into certain literary molds, or we should indeed be
speaking to our contemporaries in an unknown
tongue. Heartening to preachers — as to Christian
teachers — are the new catechisms produced in recent years by the United Church of Canada and by
the Church of Scotland (draft catechism for experi-
mental use, 1954) .

We have been assured that the gospel is rightly
proclaimed, not by historians speaking from a recon-
structed first century, nor by professional theologians
speaking from a system of organized knowledge, but
by reporters who have been commissioned by Him
whose character and activity they announce. Therefore, we need not be intimidated by the charge that
ours is " a picture-book theology." Ordinary people
need living pictures more than abstractions. Did not

James M. Barrie say that when a boy blessed with
good parents prays to God, it is the image of his
mother that appears on the retina of his soul? God
knew that, for all our boasted intellectual prowess,
we need to find the image of the invisible God in
One like ourselves. The incarnation of God in Jesus
Christ was a necessity, not only for God to make himself known, but for us, his human children.

Series of doctrinal sermons grow naturally out of
concern to clarify meanings of the faith for our people. Provided such a series is reasonably brief, and
the main points of the faith clearly indicated, the
additional preparation such sermons require is am-
ply repaid in the response of persons both within the
household of faith and outside of it. Here are titles
and texts of one minister's series on the general
theme, " What We Believe ":

1. The Double Search. What we believe
concerning God. Luke 15:20: " And he arose
and came to his father. But while he was yet
at a distance, his father saw him and had
compassion, and ran and embraced him and
kissed him."

2. The Man Who Holds the Keys. What we
believe concerning Christ. Rev. 1:17, 18: " He
laid his right hand upon me, saying, ' Fear
not, I am the first and the last, and the living
one; I died, and behold I am alive for ever
more, and I have the keys of Death and
Hades.' "

3. The Mystery of the Cross. What we be-

lieve concerning the death of Christ. Rom.
5:8: " God shows his love for us in that while
we were yet sinners Christ died for us."

4. The Good Companions. What we believe concerning the Church. Eph. 1:9, 10:
" He has made known to us . . . his purpose . . . in Christ . . . to unite all things
in him, things in heaven and things on
earth."

5. What None May Find Alone. What we
believe concerning worship. Ps. 95:6, 7: " O
come, let us worship and bow down, let us
kneel before the Lord, our Maker! For he is
our God." Matt. 18:19, 20: " If two of you
agree on earth about anything they ask, it
will be done for them by my Father in heaven.
For where two or three are gathered in my
name, there am I in the midst of them."

6. The King's Grace at the King's Table.
John 11:56: " They were looking for Jesus
and saying to one another as they stood in the
temple, ' What do you think? That he will
not come to the feast? ' "

7. The New World Symphony. What we
believe concerning society. II Peter 3:13:
" But according to his promise we wait for
new heavens and a new earth in which righteousness dwells."

8. And Still Horizons Beyond. What we believe concerning life after death. I Cor. 15:22
(Phillips) : " As members of a sinful race all
men die; as members of the Christ of God

shall all men be raised to life." Rev. 22:3, 4:
" His servants shall worship [serve] him; they
shall see his face." I John 3:2: " We shall be
like him, for we shall see him as he is."

Can we " spell out " the good news we bring in
individual sermons? Basic is the good news concerning God. " In the beginning God . . ." and at the
end, and in between and beyond the beginning and
the end, God. God, who initiated and sustains the
mysterious universe and all within it — he who is the
Ground of Being, is infinite wisdom, power, righteousness, and holy love. Why are we so sure? Not only
because of evidence in the structure and purposeful-
ness of the world around us; not only because the
wisest and best men and women of every race and
age have believed in him and were not confounded
— impressive as such testimonies are. We believe in
God, active in creation and history, and involved
with his creation because he has revealed himself to
us. He has spoken. His word has been heard. " In
many and various ways God spoke of old to our fathers by the prophets " (Heb. 1:1), and to ourselves
by reverent men of science in the laboratory, by
statesmen and philosophers, in the events of history,
and by humble folk who have been attuned to the
still, small voice of his Spirit in their souls. This
knowledge of God's reality and goodness is not the
great illusion of naïve and credulous minds. As we
did not create the facts of nature, nor invent nuclear energy, so we have not woven the idea of God
out of wishful thinking or of superstitious dread. In

life there is a " givenness " and God is the supreme
" given." A nineteenth century physicist said that
whenever he was just on the verge of making what is
called a scientific discovery, he had the strange feeling that not only was he approaching the truth, but
that quite independently the truth was from its own
side approaching him. Is this not part of what Christians mean by " revelation "? Man's search for meaning, for wholeness, for God, is always a double search.
" I girded thee though thou hast not known me " is
said to every honest seeker of God (Isa. 45:5, K.J.V.).
A sermon on " The Double Search " might well be
based on this text. Or the better known words of Job
and the psalmist: " Oh, that I knew where I might
find him . . . ! "; " Whither shall I go from thy
. . . presence? " Such a message would reproduce
our Lord's pictures of God as the seeker as well as
the sought.

But who is the God with whom we have to do?
" Who is the God of the Christians? " asked a pagan
long ago. A Christian made answer by saying, " if
thou art worthy, thou shalt know." Such an answer is
true, but it remains partial. Assuredly God cannot
reveal himself to the man who refuses to face the
truth, or who persists in denying reality to anything
except nerve-end sensations or what he grandly calls
physicochemical facts, or dialectical materialism. Jesus our Lord had nothing to say to a sly sensualist
named Herod and said nothing to him. But who can
be worthy unless God takes a hand in making him so?

Moreover, many a decent man and woman willing
to believe feel confused by the interpretations reli-

gious thinkers give. An American versifier, Phyllis
McGinley, voiced their complaint and query:

" Always on Monday, God's in the morning papers,
 His Name is a headline, His Works are rumored
  abroad.
 Having been praised by men who are movers and
  shapers,
  From prominent Sunday pulpits, newsworthy is
   God.

" On page 27, just opposite Fashion Trends
 One reads at a glance how He scolded the Bap-
  tists a little,
 Was firm with the Catholics, practical with the
  Friends,
  To Unitarians pleasantly noncommittal.
 In print are His numerous aspects, too: God smil-
  ing,
  God vexed, God thunderous, God whose man-
   sions are pearl,
 Political God, God frugal, God reconciling
  Himself with science, God guiding the Camp
   Fire Girl.

" Always on Monday morning the Press reports
 God as revealed to His vicars in various guises —
 Benevolent, stormy, patient, or out of sorts.
  But only God knows which God God recognizes."
      (" The Day After Sunday,"
    in *The Love Letters of Phyllis McGinley*) .

Which God? The God who revealed himself as holy,
righteous love, to Abraham, Moses, the prophets of

the Exile; the God who made covenant with his people Israel, an agreement written on the tablets of the
heart; the God who made his supreme self-revelation
in the historic Jesus and the risen and reigning Lord
Jesus Christ; who in Christ gathered together the
new Israel, which is his spiritual body the Church;
the God who comes in the Baby Jesus, in the Man
Christ Jesus, in the Crucified Redeemer on Calvary's
cross, in the risen and victorious Lord.

The Bible is the unique record of that double
search, a search by and for the individuals and the
community. The community of Israel realized its one-
ness and power and moved into its extraordinary mission as an instrument of redemption when it re-
sponded to God's self-revelation and offer of his
covenant to it. But revelation is more than mystical
contacts with reality through the garments of God's
natural world; more than words spoken to responsive minds; more than agreements made with ethi-
cally sensitive, spiritually acute men. Revelation is
supremely meaningful when it is made through a person. One may say, as he watches his friend come
through a terrific ordeal with gallantry and strength:
" I never knew he had it in him. It is a revelation to
me." God must have known that we should never
fully realize that he had " in him " such love and
tenderness, such invincible goodness, had he not revealed himself in the human personality of Jesus of
Nazareth. Thank God that it is the nature of love to
reveal itself. Thank God, too, that the divine Love
reveals himself, not to the " wise " and erudite, to
the sophisticate, but to those whom Jesus called
" babes."

To many who believe in God's existence, he seems so obscure and hidden that he might as well not exist, except as the noblest hypothesis by which to explain the structure of life in an orderly universe. Such persons understand the vivid analogy of John Henry Newman: It is as if a person looked into a mirror and did not see his own face to look into " this living and busy world and see no reflection of its Creator." A sermon on " The Divine Hide-and-Seek " might help such perplexed pilgrims. Isaiah 45:15 has the apposite text: " Truly, thou art a God who hidest thyself, O God of Israel, the Savior." In the religion of revelation there is that which is elusive, almost secretive, " simple to know, but mysterious to understand; sure but not plain."

> " He hides Himself so wondrously,
>   As if there were no God."
>   (Frederick W. Faber.)

God may hide himself from us in order to perfect our faith, " until we all attain to the unity of the faith and of the knowledge of the Son of God, to mature manhood, to the measure of the stature of the fullness of Christ " (Eph. 4:13). Truly the God and Father of our Lord Jesus Christ may be our Saviour because he not only makes himself known but because he hides himself.

Doubtless in the pulpit as in church councils we can express an " irreligious solicitude for God." But in a generation infected by practical atheism and in a culture increasingly secular much of our preaching may well be a witnessing to our faith in the great God

who draws near to us in Christ. "How can you believe in God in a world like this?" is a question asked
by many contemporaries. Any thoughtful believer
knows that the knowledge of God comes, not like the
solution to a problem in mathematics, but as a claim,
a challenge, a call to be obeyed. Nevertheless a reasonable statement of the case for belief may remove
certain roadblocks on the pathway to reality, down
which the Spirit may come to the soul wistful but
unconvinced. Paul's affirmation in the face of a less
sophisticated polytheism than our age knows offers
a strong text and a kind of symphonic theme for such
a sermon: "Yet for us there is one God, the Father,
from whom are all things and for whom we exist, and
one Lord, Jesus Christ, through whom are all things
and through whom we exist" (I Cor. 8:6). How can
others share this confidence?

1. *Look at the sky.* Consider the mysterious universe. A materialistic view is too simple to do justice
to the facts. It is just too naïve to say York Minster
merely happened. "Chance and change are busy
ever" but cannot explain the constitution and order
of the world. On a tablet in the Adler Planetarium in
Chicago is inscribed: "Under the great celestial fir-
mament there is order, interdependence, and unity."

2. *Look at people and the moral and spiritual
heights to which they climb as well as the depths to
which they fall.* There are plenty of scoundrels at
large; but there are also saints in the most unlikely
places. Just when you despair of this "despicable
biped" you encounter a person in whom unselfish
love and genuine nobility shine like lights in a dark

world. It takes God to account for such moral heroism and beauty.

3. *Look within yourself.* This complex personality, with its hungers which bread cannot satisfy nor human love wholly complete — this "striking novelty in a world of impersonal atoms and force" — cannot be an effect of something impersonal. And what are we to make of this sense of "oughtness," however dim or distorted it may seem? Why do men and women strive and sacrifice for "something not seen with the eyes" which they believe must be true, and with which they have dealings?

4. *Look at Jesus Christ.* If you cannot accept him as the unique Son of God, the supreme revelation of reality, can you not accept him as the best exponent of spiritual truth? Jesus believed in God, and Jesus is not just "anyone." We value expert testimony and counsel in other fields of interest. Here is One who has the right to speak concerning moral and spiritual things. From first to last he believed in God with all his being: "'I must be in my Father's house'" and "'about my Father's business.'" "'I am not alone, for the Father is with me.'" "'I seek not my own will but the will of him who sent me.'" And at journey's end, from the cross still he clung to the God whose love he disclosed and whose purpose he served: "'Father, forgive them; . . . Father, into thy hands I commit my spirit!'" God was the response that answered the faith of Jesus. God is also the loving approach from the Unseen expressed in Jesus. Such a sermon will leave men and women confronted by this God, so that some at least will be able to say from

" inside information ": " For us there is one God, the
Father, . . . and one Lord, Jesus Christ."

A different approach to this central concern of the
Christian community has been used by more than
one preacher. Instead of asking such questions as:
" How can you believe in God? " " What do you
mean by God? " or " Do we need God? ", the question put has been, " Do you really want to believe in
God? " For multitudes God is the meaning of life,
the sustainer of their lives, the companion of every
road, and their unfailing ally. But to others God can
be a divine disturber, an eternal torment, a celestial
nuisance.

The writer of Ps. 52 pictures a man who did not
want to believe in God, and waxes sarcastic about this
self-sufficient egocentric individual: " ' See the man
who would not make God his refuge, but trusted in
the abundance of his riches, and sought refuge in his
wealth! ' " (v. 7) . Such persons need not possess great
wealth to find God " the unwished for."

Certain consequences of belief in the God of Christian revelation and experience may be decidedly disturbing:

1. To believe in God means to believe in a world
of moral law, that the foundations of the universe
are laid in righteousness. Reassuring as such faith
may be when evil seems to be winning a succession
of victories, it may also be disquieting when we are
flouting certain moral laws and expect to " get away
with it." If God is holy, righteous love, it means that
in the long run nobody anywhere gets away with anything wrong. " God does not pay at the end of every

week, but in the end he pays." Belief in God makes
a man ask as Joseph did, " ' How . . . can I do this
great wickedness, and sin against God? ' " (Gen.
39:9) .

2. Do we desire to believe in God when such belief means that we and our fellow humans have endless possibilities of spiritual growth ahead of us? If
God lives, then, as Emerson said,

> " What is excellent
> As God lives, is permanent."

Comforting this may be to one whose dearest has vanished at death's touch; disturbing it may be if it
means that we should live the kind of life that deserves to continue beyond physical death. If life is
brutish and short, I need not worry too much about
my failures.

3. Do we want to believe in God when such belief
imposes an obligation to live like the sons and daughters of the Highest? Religion, like patriotism, may be
the refuge of the selfish, even of the scoundrel; but
great religion sends a man out to live above the average and ahead of his time for Christ's sake. Vitally to
believe in God, to confide all of ourselves to all that
we know of God in our Lord Jesus Christ, is to join
God in his creation of a commonwealth of sons and
daughters, like him in character, and seeking to master the resources of God's creation for the benefit of
all his human family. Before such a sermon is done,
some hearers will find themselves wanting the key of
intelligible faith, the tremendous stimulus, and the
unfailing security that belief in the God and Father

of the Lord Jesus Christ bestows. For, despite the sinfulness of human beings, there is a slumbering hero in every soul God has made. And God seeks to release that heroic spirit and restore his child to himself and the divine family. Given the response of love and obedience, the Spirit enables a person to say honestly and without conceit, as Martin Luther said, " God knows me right well, and I know him not ill."

III. "*Only Like Souls I See the Folk . . .*"

(To Whom Do We Preach?)

Elizabeth Barrett Browning said of Thomas Carlyle that he "knocked out his window from the blind wall of his century" (*E. B. Browning,* a biography by Dorothy Hewlett, p. 14). Through that window he saw in new perspective the portents and personalities of his time. Consequently he spoke to his contemporaries with vehemence and authority in what Mrs. Browning called "soul language." As interpreter of the timeless Word of God to men, the Christian preacher must knock windows out of the blind walls of his century. We have a duty to understand not only the truth of Christ, but the world of persons to which we would direct it. Jesus our Lord blazed indignantly at men who could interpret natural phenomena and failed to understand the human situation. "You frauds!" he exclaimed. "You know how to interpret the look of the earth and the sky. Why can't you interpret the meaning of the times in which you live?" (Luke 12:56, in *The Gospels,* translated by J. B. Phillips). He did not need to have anyone tell him what was in man or what were the trends of society. He expected us to be perceptive.

A common criticism of the man in the pulpit fastens on his alleged isolation from the real world. If such criticism is at all justified, the minister's study must become a room with a view. The minister himself would better strive to see the contemporary scene and its human actors as steadily and whole as the eyes of his mind and soul permit. Something like bifocal lenses would help. Scripture warns against being content either with long-sightedness or with its opposite. " The eyes of a fool are on the ends of the earth " (Prov. 17:24) . He overlooks the treasure in his own back yard and is blind to what remotely controlled forces are doing to those by his side. Conversely the victim of spiritual myopia, who never raises his sights to far horizons, is equally handicapped. " For whoever lacks these things " — knowledge and brotherly affection as well as faith and virtue — " is blind and shortsighted and has forgotten that he was cleansed from his old sins " (II Peter 1:9) .

Oculists are not lacking to correct our limited or distorted vision. Social scientists, philosophers, theologians offer their services that we may see and understand our age. Some of them act as small-sized seismographs registering the moral earthquakes of our era and forecasting probable developments. Recall current descriptions of our time, some of them in danger of becoming stereotypes. This, said W. H. Auden, is " the age of anxiety," peopled by

> " Children afraid of the night
> Who have never been happy or good."

An American sociologist has joined the psychologists labeling our generation, " the age of loneliness," and urban citizens of at least the Western hemisphere, " the lonely crowd." Since 1945 we have been reluctant and apprehensive members of the atomic age. " We are living in an age of disorder and upheaval," writes Mr. Walter Lippmann (*Atlantic* magazine, May, 1954). One recent observer of Western society offers another designation, " The Age of Publicity," in which the two key figures are the press agent and the psychoanalyst. As a result, he finds us increasingly regimented, conformists to substandard concepts and codes. Yet an age of publicity and of mass communication has even uglier accompaniments. Men are aliens to one another. Neighbor distrusts neighbor, seeing him as a potential heretic or traitor. So not surprisingly ours is called " the age of suspicion." Said the second Assembly of the World Council of Churches, it is a time of ferment in which " there are both hopes and fears." Here is a more detailed description which conceivably might appeal to future historians as a judicious appraisal of our era:

" It was the best of times, it was the worst of times;
It was the age of wisdom, it was the age of foolishness;
It was the epoch of belief, it was the epoch of incredulity;
It was the season of light, it was the season of darkness;
It was the spring of hope, it was the winter of despair;

We had everything before us: we were all going direct

To heaven, we were all going direct the other way."

But those lines were written by Charles Dickens in 1859 to describe the year 1775 (*A Tale of Two Cities*). Are we, then, to conclude with the ancient Preacher that "what has been is what will be, and what has been done is what will be done" (Eccl. 1:9) ; that men live forever on Futility Street, doomed to frustration, weariness, defeat? Christians cannot accept such unrelieved pessimism as a true reading of any time because "something new has been added." God has visited and redeemed his people in the Lord Jesus Christ. In a sermon on the question, "What Is Your View of Life? ", a man may help his people to face the two alternatives memorably set down in our Bible:

1. The view of the cynical pagan — "all things come alike to all: there is one event to the righteous, and to the wicked; to the good " and to the evil (Eccl. 9:2, K.J.V.).

2. The conviction of the Christian realist: "All things work for . . . good," or, if you prefer the Revised Standard Version, "We know that in everything God works for good with those who love him, who are called according to his purpose" (Rom. 8:28).

Such descriptions by our social analysts prove illuminating as we examine the spiritual climate in which we and our people live. We shall be excused if we have moments when we think the salesclerk's conclusion was sound. Asked by a young mother if

the toy he recommended was not rather complicated
for a small child, he answered: " It's an educational
toy, madam, designed to help the child adjust himself to the world of today. Any way he puts it together is wrong." That salesman's attitude is characteristic of many moderns as they contemplate the
chaos within and around them. Five-year plans, ten-
year plans, elaborate schemes of one kind and another
on national and international levels are proposed
and, when tried, achieve at best disappointingly
meager success. Commentators on the contemporary
human scene frequently speak of the disillusionment
that infects the earth's inhabitants. In his disturbed
generation Jeremiah did not ignore the sorry scheme
of things, but he heard and transmitted the reassuring word of the divine Architect and Master Builder:
" For I know the plans I have for you, says the Lord,
plans for welfare and not for evil, to give you a future
and a hope " (Jer. 29:11) .

If we would lead people to the place where they
can meet Him in whom is their future and their
hope, we must do more than study the findings of
even expert diagnosticians. Professor Gordon Allport,
Harvard University psychologist, points the direction. Perhaps the basic principle of the science of human relations, he said, is that in order to deal effectively with any other mortal it is necessary to find out
how he feels. To deal effectively with our fellow mortals to whom we preach, it is imperative that we know
how they feel. Like Ezekiel — but it is to be hoped
without his bitter reluctance and for longer than a
week — we must go among our people, so many of

them exiles from their homeland in God (Ezek.
3:15) . Only as we faithfully exercise our cure of souls
— patiently and persistently engage in adventures of
understanding their inner hungers and frustrations,
their fears and hopes; learn something of the social
context in which they work and play — do we gain
such knowledge. A veteran newspaperman was asked
by his editor why he experienced difficulty in rewrit-
ing a reporter's factual account of a particular incident. He explained by saying, " I have not lived myself into the story." Only as we live ourselves into the
story of the individuals in our parish can we interpret their needs, and the gospel in the light of them.
Some of the most profound truths ever uttered were
spoken by Jesus to a strange woman whom he met at
a wellside. What stabbed her broad awake was his
penetrating insight into her own soul. He swiftly
lived himself into her story, uncovered the causes
of her moral sickness. Despite the evasiveness she
adroitly employed, she was compelled to face herself.
As a result, she forgot why she came to the well and
rushed to her neighbors crying, " Come, see a man
who told me all that I ever did " (John 4:1–30) .
Without prejudice to divine omniscience, may we not
say reverently that even our Lord's ministry to individuals and to crowds derived much of its sharp relevance from his constant intimate contacts with persons?

For Christ's minister there can be no substitute for
person-to-person relationship. Nor does a time come
when the mystery of a human personality is completely unraveled, neatly catalogued, and filed for

ready reference. As Mr. T. S. Eliot's " confidential
clerk " observed:

" There's no end to understanding a person —
   All one can do is to understand them better
   To keep up with them; so that as the other changes
   You can understand the change as soon as it hap-
      pens,
   Though you couldn't have predicted it.

" There's always something one's ignorant of
   About anyone, however well one knows them;
   And that may be something of the greatest impor-
      tance.
   It's when you're sure you understand a person
   That you're liable to make the worst mistake about
      him."

When he learned that I intended leaving the parish
ministry for one devoted to teaching future ministers,
the late Lloyd C. Douglas, a popular American novelist, wrote me a characteristic note of encouragement.
In it he gently warned me against yielding to a temptation to which academics are vocationally suscep-
tible. It is the tendency to forget that there are people
living " on the other side of the tracks," common folk
neither possessing nor desiring the advantages of
cloistered scholarship and sheltered piety. If I walk
with scholarly kings nor lose the common touch, I
must avoid as I would the devil, he said, moving into
a private world of ideas and abstractions. Such a
world is likely to be insulated against the sound and
fury of factories and shops as well as soundproofed

against "the still, sad music of humanity." It is
sound counsel for those uncharitably described as
" refugees from the pastorate." The cautionary word
also deserves serious thought by those on the front
line of the Church's service who would make their
studies or the local church program a kind of foxhole
or dugout when distracting and demanding human
beings draw near. He who called us to be His ministers not only looked with compassion upon the mul-
titude; he sought them out, lived with them, identified himself completely with them in their need and
sin, and loved them to the end and beyond. We are
not Christ, but by God's grace we are " in Christ,"
and therefore committed to his kind of compassion-
ate service to individuals in their known needs.

Understanding of a person involves not only patient, responsive listening born of the love that in
Christ hopes all things. Interpretations of the temper
and probabilities of the age in which the person lives,
while immensely helpful, are also insufficient. A further strategy must be followed: To learn how the individuals in our congregations feel, we must become
familiar with the context of their daily work. Then
it becomes easier to sense the pressures — economic,
political, social — to which they are subjected. One
of Charles Dickens' characters was said to possess
the key to the street. Christ's minister should be
similarly equipped. Is he not one of that high company to which is entrusted the keys of the Kingdom?
If a man loves God and loves those for whom he was
content to give the Son of his love, he will do in his
own fashion throughout his ministry what Dick Shep-

pard did one memorable night before he began his
London pastorate. Previous to his induction as vicar
of St. Martin's-in-the-Fields, that unconventional
saint of radiant memory spent an entire night exploring the parish and neighborhood of his new church.
" I went into many a strange building until then unknown to me," he recalled. " And I talked to all who
would talk to me. I was in a Casualty Ward at Char-
ing Cross Hospital, without being a casualty, and the
courts of Bedfordbury, as well as several public
houses, for the first time; and, thinking in those days
that the Embankment was in the parish, I spent several hours on its benches, ending up in the early
morning at a coffee stall close to the church. . . . It
was this night's impressions that persuaded me that
no square mile could provide a more thrilling and
adventurous pitch for a parson's job " (R. Ellis Rob-
erts, *H. R. L. Sheppard*). One may add that it was
this night's impressions and those gained on many
subsequent days and nights spent among his fellow
men that persuaded many of his previously indiffer-
ent parishioners that when Dick Sheppard preached
his deceptively simple sermons, he spoke God's truth
to persons he knew and loved for Christ's sake and
their own. As preparation for sermon making and the
actual world of persons, pity that man who

> " Neither moteless nor beamless,
>   But sightless [has] the eye
>   *That sees things and not people*."

Though I possess vast technical knowledge of so-
ciology, psychology, political economy, so that I can

speak correctly the impressive jargon of pundits in
these fields, and have not the love which leads into
creative personal contacts with people, I amount to
nothing at all as a preacher of Christ. If I have that
absolute faith and competence in dialectical theology
so that I can confound the intellectuals and impress
examiners of candidates for the highest academic de-
grees, but " couldn't care less " what my parishioners
were up against in their families, their jobs, their
leisure, and their inner lives, I should achieve pre-
cisely nothing in my preaching. For this love seeks a
way of helping individuals to help themselves in the
power of God's Spirit. " It is neither anxious to impress nor does it cherish inflated ideas of its own im-
portance." This Christlike love knows " no end to its
trust, no fading of its hope: it can outlast anything "
(last two sentences from J. B. Phillips' paraphrase of
I Cor., ch. 13) .

Entrusted with the gospel as we are; finding in
companionship with our Lord incentive and resource
to be shepherds who know their flock and the forces
that mold their lives, as we do, how do we see those
to whom we preach? Modern preachers may not relish
the role, but, like the prophets of ancient Israel, they
must be assayers and testers of God's people (cf. Jer.
6:27) .

(1) Let us locate them within our society. *Those
to whom most of us preach are* bracketed by sociolo-
gists *within the middle class.* Hierarchical structure
of society rightly may be distasteful to us, carrying
connotations of a rigid caste system which deserves
the disintegration that has overtaken it in many com-

munities. Yet even in democratic nations, and in
spite of changes in the past fifty years, lower, middle,
and upper classes, with their various gradations, persist. With noteworthy exceptions such as inner city
churches and industrial parishes, our white Protestant congregations in North America are predomi-
nantly middle class. A similar condition apparently
prevails elsewhere. One of the final statements approved by the 1954 Assembly of the World Council
of Churches emphasized the " need to change the
[church] atmosphere . . . of an old-fashioned, middle-class culture." Rightly the same message on the
laity deplored " a tendency to choose the lay leader-
ship of a congregation from among white-collar workers " since it " often prevents others, especially young
industrial workers, from feeling at home in the
church." Nevertheless the fact remains that most of
our congregations in towns and cities are composed
of middle-class persons. They belong to the " white-
collar " group. This large group consists of the workers who perform the major routines of our society.
One has said that the world as they know it looks
like " a great salesroom, an enormous filing cabinet,
an incorporated brain, a new universe of manage-
ment and manipulation." The same astute observer
finds the white-collar man " pushed by forces beyond
his control, pulled into movements he does not understand . . . getting into situations in which his is
the most helpless position " (C. Wright Mills, *White
Collar*) . The middle-class person faces troubles common to all men and women living in the second half
of the twentieth century. He has been racked by eco-

nomic depression, war, monetary inflation, and by the
threat of another more frightful and futile global
war. George Orwell's Mr. Bowling, a salesman in his
novel *Coming Up for Air,* voices the complaint of
the group when he says, " There's a lot of rot talked
about the sufferings of the working class. I'm not
sorry for the proles myself. . . . The prole suffers
physically, but he's a free man when he isn't working.
But in every one of those little stucco homes there
is some poor _____ who's never free except when
he's fast asleep and dreaming that he's got the boss
down the bottom of a well and is bunging lumps of
coal at him. Of course, the basic trouble with people like us is that we all imagine we've got something to lose." Mr. C. Wright Mills, author of one
of the penetrating studies of the new middle class in
America describes " the new Little Man's " plight
convincingly: he " seems to have no firm roots, no
sure loyalties to sustain his life and give it a center. . . . Perhaps because he does not know where
he is going, he is in a frantic hurry; perhaps because
he does not know what frightens him, he is paralyzed
with fear." In his political life (and the parish minister may suspect, in his religious life as well), this
paralysis results in a profound apathy. Any pastor
realizes that deep uneasiness characterizes many such
individuals. Confirming the minister's opinion, the
sociologist explains that the malaise disturbing many
of his parishioners may be traced to the loss of the
certainties by which earlier generations lived. Jesus
was sure that the cause of recurring uneasiness and
distress was due to their rootlessness: " They have no

root in themselves," he said. When trouble comes, they give up (Mark. 4:17). We speak to many who lack great beliefs, follow no master plan for living, and therefore show " no acceptance and no rejection, no sweeping hope and no sweeping rebellion." A modern poet, Lora Dunetz, speaks mordantly of such a representative of the white-collar group in her lines " While the Bells Ring ":

" Pursuer, eluder,
  Lying in wait at the snare or evading the trap,
  Afraid of the sharp, the sudden, the accidental,
  Man, the great carnivore, daily on the hunt
  In the forest or market place for the not-fleet-
    enough,
  Sits in the semishade of his veranda on Sunday,
  Comforted by the second warmth of the coffee,
  At peace with his world, his house, his self,
  And turns from an editorial presaging the doom of
    the species
  While the bells ring praises."

God has given us a word to speak to such outwardly smug souls, " men with blinkered eyes and hobbled feet " who grope " down a narrow groove and call it life." It is a word that will shatter their complacency by its revelation of their plight, increase their turbulence of mind, until at last they take themselves to the place where " the bells ring praises " of One who gives the forgiveness and newness of life that will make their trivial escapes from sordid and selfish weekday struggle as unnecessary as they are unworthy.

(2) As a " white-collar " man, the person to whom we speak is more likely to be *a city man* than a country man. In fact, because of modern means of transportation and communication, the rural citizen himself is more likely to be increasingly urban, if not urbane, in his attitudes and way of life. Cities may be malignant growths on the body of civilization, but they do exert a powerful appeal to human beings. Job opportunities, the chance of getting ahead, educational advantages, entertainment possibilities, all are present to a degree not found in villages or countryside. But it is commonplace to say that cities do things, many of them harmful, to those who live and work in them. Mr. Auden's searching discussion of the age of anxiety takes place in a city " pub " (*The Age of Anxiety.* A Baroque Eclogue) . Choice of such a setting was not capricious. Within the oppressing city, men seek a liquid nirvana or some other kind. Pushed, compressed, tempted, deprived, the city man craves some means to endure the harsh and lonely existence of *urbs* and factory. One who long served as Christ's minister in one of our greatest cities draws a picture of the city man in these terms: lonely, confused, insecure, empty, anxious. Are we surprised to learn that trustworthy statistics prove that a higher rate of personality disintegration occurs in our cities than in the country? that the best sellers among nonfiction books in America for many months recently have been guides to confident living based on simple suggestions whereby the reader may tap the power of positive thinking? We may decry reducing the gospel to techniques to induce peace of mind, and rightly

declare the peril of modernizing Christ so that he becomes a twentieth century psychotherapist. But we
cannot ignore the element of response to messages in
pulpits and books addressed to people who live under
tensions and desire release from them.

Our city man and woman live in crowds. Personal
anonymity envelops them like a chilling fog, and
through it they are stalked by a gray ghost, loneliness, and its murderous comrade, despair. An exiled
Scot who shared my lodgings on a student mission
field in Alberta told me that he felt lonelier standing
near the entrance to a great city's huge department
store than he ever felt on the vast western Canadian
prairies where only an occasional light in a farm-
house window denoted human habitation. Like the
desolate psalmist (Ps. 142:4), my friend was sure that
no man cared for his soul, or — unless a traffic acci-
dent laid him low — for his body either. Christ and
Christ's people are here to banish loneliness, to in-
troduce the solitary to the family of God. Let the
preacher speak on " Christ's Conquest of Loneliness,"
taking his text from such a saying as Jesus' " Alone
. . . yet . . . not alone, for the Father is with me! "
— showing how this Friend of all the friendless longs
to impart his secret, eagerly welcomes the homesick
and unwanted — and he will find astonishing response. If in such a message he rouses his own members to act, in church and out of it, as a genuine
society of friends to the shy stranger, the uprooted
newcomer, the Church comes alive as a dynamic, redemptive fellowship, translating the Word preached
into creative deed. The outsiders will know that they

" are no longer strangers and sojourners, but . . .
fellow citizens with the saints and members of the
household of God " (Eph. 2:19) .

(3) Many of those to whom we preach, therefore,
are anxious, lonely, and confused. Men have always
been. But a further fact has made the anxiety and
fear assume aggravated, endemic proportions. It is
the dreadful fact of the nuclear bomb's killing potential. True, in order to transact daily business and
live in any tolerable fashion, men cannot constantly
think of the menace. But it is there — a black, in-
fernal cloud on the horizon of all our life. It is probably exaggeration to say that on every Bible and book
we read, on every article of clothing we wear, rests an
infinitesimal particle of radioactive dust. It is not fan-
tastic to say that much of the gnawing anxiety destroying men's peace is traceable to what happened
in 1945, when the atomic bomb was dropped on Japa-
nese cities, and again in 1954, when the hydrogen
bomb was successfully tested. Brittle in their humor
and with an overtone of typically modern fatalism
are these lines which appeared in *The New Yorker*
(April 10, 1954) a month after the H-bomb exploded
in the Pacific:

" When you hear the sound and see the flash
   Don't duck under the nearest table,
   'Cause there won't be any table;
   Don't pull the tablecloth over you,
   'Cause there won't be any tablecloth;
   Don't throw yourself flat on the floor,
   'Cause there won't be any floor;

And don't, under any circumstances, try to leave the
  city,
'Cause there won't be any city left to leave.
Simply pause for a moment to adjust your shroud
And make your way leisurely to the nearest cloud "
                  (Frances Minturn Howard) .

How are we to speak to individuals who cannot be
so nonchalant in the face of unimaginably dire disaster? Jeremiah's black depression may be our mood:
" Gather together, let us go into the fortified cities
and perish there " (Jer. 8:14) . In the light of the incarnation, atonement, and resurrection of Christ, we
cannot say confidently with the same prophet " the
Lord our God has doomed us to perish, and has given
us poisoned water to drink, because we have sinned
against the Lord." But his reflection rings true today
as when he wrote: " We looked for peace, but no
good came, for a time of healing, but behold, terror "
(v. 15) . As Paul Tillich observed, ancient prophecy
has become modern physics. Is not a sermon on
" Good News for Those Afraid of the Future " indicated? Four notes of Christian assurance can be
sounded:

(a.) Assurance of our value to God. Man is so
greatly loved by his Creator and Redeemer that an-
nihilation of the total personality is unthinkable:
" God so loved the world that he gave his only Son "
(John 3:16) .

(b.) Assurance of the soul's safety in God. Whatever comes, our security is in Christ, whose loving
power expels the fear of " ' those who kill the body,

and after that have no more that they can do ' "
(Luke 12:4).

(c.) Assurance that a sure way out is available.
Making God's Kingdom of fraternal righteousness
and just peace our top priority on every level of human affairs is the only road to obtain all else that we
need to avert collective suicide (Matt. 6:33).

(d.) Assurance that in the death and resurrection
of Christ the ultimate victory has been won in advance — " having drawn the sting of all the powers
ranged against us, He exposed them, shattered, empty
and defeated, in His final glorious triumphant act! "
(Col. 2:15, Phillips).

(4) The white-collar man or the man in overalls
or battle dress, living in towns and cities and countryside in this atomic age — do we really understand
him until we see him as a child of God who has lost
his way? The Bible puts it bluntly: " All have sinned
and fall short of the glory of God " (Rom. 3:23).
For us the final and authoritative estimate of man,
of the people to whom we preach, is that made by
our Lord. He had no illusions about human nature.
" He himself knew what was in man." His estimate
was neither romantically high nor despairingly low.
More than once he described individuals and groups
as if they were spawned in hell. From the souls of the
so-called best people he tore the masks of pretension:
" You hypocrites, you brood of vipers, you white-
washed tombs, you offspring of Satan," — how his
words burn and sear the " holy Willies," " the unco
guid " of his day and ours! Nor did he sentimentalize
over the virtues of the proletariat. " This evil generation " was one of his phrases for the rank and file.

No psychiatric depth analysis goes deeper than his own reading of the black depths of the human soul: "' From within, out of the heart of man, come evil thoughts, fornication, theft, murder, adultery, coveting, wickedness, deceit, licentiousness, envy, slander, pride, foolishness. All these evil things come from within, and they defile a man ' " (Mark 7:21–23). Not from Christ did Swinburne or any other bland humanist learn to chant, " Glory to man in the highest! for man is the master of things." Nor did this divine realist hesitate to brand as evil entire communities or corporate groups: "' Woe to you, Chorazin! woe to you, Bethsaida! . . . it shall be more tolerable on the day of judgment for Tyre and Sidon than for you. And you, Capernaum, . . . shall be brought down to Hades ' " (Matt. 11:21–23). (Imagine the popularity rating of the preacher who used such language about London, Washington, Moscow, Paris, or Peiping!) As for the total picture, he painted it in somber reds and blacks. One who faithfully reflected his mind asserted that " the whole world is in the power of the evil one " (I John 5:19). Jesus acknowledged that the demonic would have its hour of triumph, and that the hour would seem unconscionably long. Never did he minimize life's tragic element: "' In the world you have tribulation ' " (John 16:33). In a world such as this, loyalty to the highest is often rewarded with misunderstanding, vile slander, persecution, and, at the end of a dark road, with a cross. Yet this same man was sure that with God all things are possible, even the transformation of God's rebellious, demon-ridden children. No one held such confidence in pitifully ordinary men's capabilities as did Jesus. He recognized the tragedy of man's fallenness but knew that he could restore him to his true status, dignity, and joy. Men, he said, are like silly, stubborn sheep. God's children become lost with many kinds of lostness — like a coin out of circulation in a dark corner; like a sheep strayed into a deep thicket; like a wayward lad in a far country mistaking self-indulgence for self-realization (Luke, ch. 15). He saw each man or woman as, not just a "wrinkled sack of pains," but as desperately sick; to such critically ill members of the family, and not to the robust he was sent, he said. He never doubted that, given the response of trust in the divine Physician, they could be completely cured. Treatment of such deep trouble must itself be radical. No frantic efforts by the patient would help; no quickly applied poultices of easy affirmations that everything is perfectly lovely if we keep looking on the bright side and exhibit self-confidence could reach the condition. He is not the leader of a cult of reassurance. After major surgery of repentance would come God's own blood transfusion of forgiving grace. God's love personalized in Christ Jesus alone works the deep therapy that will create the miracle. And it did. And it does. Persuaded that his people should realize something of the wonder of this love in Christ, one preacher urged his congregation to "see what love the Father has given us" (John 3:1a) in three 'dimensions': God's love, he said, (1) never lets us off. Calvary is proof that forgiveness is not cheap nor easy; (2) never lets us down. His grace is sufficient for every crisis and for the long, steep climb of ordi-

nary days; (3) never lets us go. Love's tenacity out-
lasts all our fickleness and holds us safely through
"death's cold, sullen stream." (These memorable
"heads" occurred in a sermon by Raymond E. Bal-
comb, D.D.) Is anyone surprised who in imagination has watched the clinics of Christ shown in the
New Testament? After the Saviour of men van-
quished death and the worst that men could do to
him, a man who had himself experienced and wit-
nessed in others Christ's power set it down as an in-
controvertible fact that "to all who received him,
who believed in his name, he gave power to become
children of God" (John 1:12). No wonder that
Christ's realistic and yet hopeful interpretation of
man in his sinfulness and in his potential splendor
created a new ethic! But first it was, as it remains,
the best news for every man.

So we see those to whom we are sent with this gospel as members of the vast middle section of human
society, living in crowds but frequently as lonely,
anxious, confused, or complacent citizens of the
atomic age. But we see them most truly through the
eyes of Christ as human beings for whom Christ died,
unable themselves to end their alienation from the
Father but by his grace capable of becoming sons and
daughters of God.

"Only like souls I see the folk thereunder,
   Bound who should conquer, slaves who should be
      kings "
                  (Frederick W. H. Meyers, *Saint Paul*).

IV. "*Seek Him in the Kingdom of Anxiety*"
— W. H. Auden

At a recent summer conference the minister of a rural parish heard a series of lectures by the eminent theologian Dr. Paul Tillich. The country pastor was deeply impressed and stimulated. He was edified and at times mystified. At the conclusion he made an amusing comment: " I always knew that something was wrong with me," he said wryly. " Now I know what it is: my ontology is truncated." If they knew the meaning of the terms, many twentieth century persons might confess to being in a similar plight. Something vital is missing from their working philosophy concerning life's essential meaning. This deficiency may not be a cause of the anxiety which, according to one psychologist (Rollo May), characterizes our age more than any other period since the breakdown of the Middle Ages; but it must be a contributing factor. Dr. Tillich himself speaks of the anxiety of meaninglessness as one of the three types of anxiety caused by what he calls the threat of non-being. The other forms of " existential anxiety " are described as the anxiety of condemnation or guilt

and the anxiety of death. " Existential anxiety " is
defined as that which belongs to existence as such and
not that which reflects an abnormal state of mind
as in neurotic anxiety (Paul Tillich, *The Courage
to Be*).

Such an analysis should keep us from healing the
hurt of God's people lightly. Assuredly Christian
faith is the sovereign cure of worry, and men and
women today need to be shown how to practice this
faith. So Christ would say to his followers today what
he said to his disciples in Palestine nineteen centuries
ago: " Don't worry . . . ' What shall we eat, what
shall we drink or what shall we wear.' "! That is what
pagans are always looking for; your Heavenly Father
knows that you need them all. Set your heart on His
Kingdom and His goodness, and all these things will
come to you as matter of course.

" ' Don't worry at all then about tomorrow ' "
(Matt. 6:25, 32–34, Phillips). But this word was spoken to men and women already " in," resolved to live
as citizens of God's Kingdom. Too frequently we
speak smooth things concerning peace of mind to
those who may need to experience further turbulence
of mind before they are ready to accept the deep
therapy of God's love. Concerning one of the most
" successful " preachers to worried moderns, it has
been said that in his version of the gospel faith is a
skill that brings usefulness and satisfaction to the
user; faith is a self-help technique. In using this technique to obtain what you want, you must never admit evil or guilt or sin; this would be " negative "
and destructive of self-confidence. One of my young

friends, a keen theological thinker, is sure that this kind of utilitarian religion makes the church a kind of service station, prayer an efficient result-producing device, the Bible a compendium of practical techniques and formulas. Therefore, any resemblance to the Christian gospel is coincidental and mysteriously providential! Christian faith operates at a far deeper level, and releases power for radical transformation of the self. To those whose anxiety stems from a sense of meaninglessness, it speaks from depth. Deep calls unto deep.

Not long ago in a neighborhood drugstore (chemist's shop to a Briton) a middle-aged woman employed as a salesclerk told me of a local tragedy. A young widowed mother and her two children were burned to death the previous night. " Makes you wonder what life's all about, doesn't it? " said the woman. " It doesn't make sense." What *is* life all about? A major personal disaster is not needed to make many contemporaries question the ultimate destiny of things. As believers, we affirm with Paul that " life means Christ to me " (Phil. 1:21, Moffatt) . In him we find the key to life's meaning. In our preaching we must " spell it out." Generally, allegorical treatment of parables is a dubious method of interpretation. Yet allegorical use of the parable of the Pounds, as Luke reports it (ch. 19:11–27) furnishes what may prove to be a memorable means of answering the question, " What's life all about? " in terms of the Christian reading of history and of the immediate human situation. Four divisions or " heads " emerge without overmuch prodding:

1. The fact of the divine initiative. "'A noble-man [God in Christ] went into a far country [the world of men] to receive kingly power.'" At the heart of existence is power, wisdom, and love, purposeful and personal. History is truly "His story."

2. The fact of the divine grace. "'Calling . . . his servants, he gave them ten pounds, and said to them, "Trade with these till I come."'" What is there that we have not received? Life, talent, years, capacity to love and to be loved, faith, and supremely God's gift of himself. Our responsibility in the light of this "given-ness."

3. The fact of man's rebellion and the divine sacrifice to overcome it. "'But his citizens hated him and sent an embassy after him, saying, "We do not want this man to reign over us."'" The cross of Calvary is the symbol of our resistance and the sign of God's action to overcome it.

4. The fact of divine judgment and human accountability. "When he returned, having received the kingly power, he commanded these servants, to whom he had given the money, to be called to him, that he might know what they had gained by trading." He still comes in judgment, and the Church's faith declares that he will come at history's end or beyond it. "What did you make of it?" remains his question. As the Cockney soldier heard in his dream, the divine Judge asks, "Well?" Here the analogy breaks down. Unlike the nobleman in Jesus' story, the great God whom Jesus reveals cannot ruthlessly destroy his enemies like some Oriental despot. But his love comes in judgment and in mercy's name pre-

scribing surgical treatment which might make sudden extinction almost preferable.

> " And then at last, 'E said one word,
>   'E just said one word — ' Well? '
>   And I said in a funny voice,
>   ' Please can I go to hell? '

> " And then 'E answered, ' No, you can't,
>   That hell is for the blind,
>   And not for those that see.
>   You know that you have earned it, lad,
>   So you must follow Me.
>   Follow Me on by the paths of pain,
>   Seeking what you have seen,
>   Until at last you can build the " Is "
>   With the brick of the " Might Have Been." '

.   .   .   .

> " I've got to follow what I've seen
>   Till this old body dies:
>   For I daren't face in the land o' grace
>   The sorrow o' those eyes."

" ' A nobleman went into a far country to receive
kingly power and then return.' " This makes sense of
" this ambiguous earth," but only when we let Him
take his kingly power over and within us. No better
Scripture for a sermon on the Final Judgment may be
found than the familiar parable of the Sheep and the
Goats (Matt. 25:31–46). (As John Huxtable, D.D.,
Principal of New College, Hampstead, pointed out
in a university sermon at Cambridge, the story indi-
cates: (1) the way in which the judgment will be

given; (2) the standards by which we shall be judged; (3) the sort of people who will be among the sheep and who among the goats.) " The real tragedy of the story is not that some are dismissed to whatever fate the words ' eternal punishment ' describe, but that they have heard addressed to them the most awful words anyone may dread to hear: ' Depart from me.' " — *The Cambridge Review*, January 29, 1955, p. 311.

As for the anxiety of guilt, it may be that theologians and preachers exaggerate its prevalence. After all, we have been emancipated from much morbid concern with sin. But is a sense of guilt unknown except in hypersensitive personalities unfortunately damaged by a certain type of religious teaching in their impressionable years? Arnold Bennett, militantly secularist in his philosophy, experienced something close to it. In his last illness, and in spite of his success as a novelist, he expressed a sense of failure and defeat. Turning to Dorothy Cheston Bennett, he said, " Everything has gone wrong, my girl."

What do we make of accusing memories? of the sense of guilt which appears to have disturbed many of our generation's ablest scientists such as nuclear physicists? No person who realistically views the human situation and examines his own inner life and personal history can deny that something has gone wrong with man. We know it, and we know that the deep " fallenness " is more than incomplete growth toward maturity. Some years ago Sir Winston Churchill saw what optimistic churchmen of the period failed to see, that the " root error of utopian idealism is its failure to take a sufficiently tragic view of human nature." No man who hears confessions of troubled souls, be he priest or minister, consulting psychologist or physician, minimizes the amount of anxiety traceable to guilt or self-condemnation. When William Booth surveyed the slums of the city, he exclaimed, " How I hate the enemy who has wrought this havoc! " Notwithstanding the noteworthy improvement in social conditions, the enemy's operations continue in all sectors. In the first and second chapters of The Book of Job there is an unexpectedly vivid reference to the ubiquity of moral evil. In the narrative it is a kind of stage direction: " Now there was a day when the sons of God came to present themselves before the Lord, and Satan also came among them " (Job 1:6; 2:1). It is as if a reporter described a meeting of the General Assembly's officers, or the House of Bishops, and then added: " The president of the Association for the Advancement of Atheism was seated next to the moderator, or next to the archbishop of Canterbury! " To give it an American parallel, it would be as if a Congressional Committee to Investigate Subversive Tendencies met in secret session and the premier of the U.S.S.R. came also. " Satan Among the Saints " sounds like a " whodunit " title, but the theme may be indicated. What of Screwtape's operatives working as undercover agents among church members? — operatives such as Snobbishness, Unbelief, and the agent who may be called Felix, since he is always counseling deferment of discipleship (Acts, ch. 24, particularly vs. 25–27).

More poignant is the deep anxiety of unresolved

guilt gnawing at the consciences of more individuals than we suspect. The prevalence of this condition may not be apparent to the casual observer. In America he may be deceived into thinking that breast-beating has been replaced by back-slapping. Doubtless it is true that many, if not a majority, of our citizens never see themselves as despicably wicked or as permanently lost. Said a recent essayist: " For all his wrestling matches with conscience, the average American . . . feels that he will turn good with age, exactly as that someday he will retire and see the world " (Louis Kronenberger, *Company Manners,* A Cultural Inquiry Into American Life) . Some years ago the American playwright Eugene O'Neill produced a somber drama entitled *Mourning Becomes Electra.* As the title indicated, he had gone back to the ancient Greek legend of Electra. In the play he unfolded the tragic story of sin in one family. Lavinia, the central figure in the play, wrestles desperately with the doom which engulfs her. She seeks a love that will save her from the poison of her passion and guilt. Clasping her lover in her arms, she cries: " We'll be happy. I love everything that grows simply — up toward the sun — everything that's straight and strong. I hate what's warped, and twists and eats into itself, and dies for a lifetime in shadow." Human beings in their moments of clear seeing do hate what " twists and eats into itself," and yearn intensely to be free. Christian faith insists that we cannot escape from this cancerous growth until we face our moral failure, our alienation from God and our fellows, and let the divine surgeon deal with our trouble. " If we are silly enough to refuse to admit that we are sinners, then we live in a world of illusion, and truth becomes a stranger to us. But if we freely admit that we have sinned, we find God utterly reliable and straightforward — he forgives our sins and makes us thoroughly clean from all that is evil. For if we take up the attitude, ' we have not sinned,' we flatly deny God's diagnosis of our condition and cut ourselves off from what He has to say to us " (I John 1:8–10, Phillips).

During the First World War, a poet pictured a sensitive, honest soldier keeping rendezvous with death but first turning to Christ in Flanders and praying:

" ' And so we ask for courage, strength and pardon —
    Especially, I think, we ask for pardon —
    And that You'll stand beside us to the last.' "

It would be beside the mark to assume that large numbers of present-day soldiers or civilians pray in such fashion. Yet many more of our contemporaries than before Hiroshima and the H-bomb tests could make such a prayer their own. If men and women do not ask: " What must I do to be saved? " " Is there forgiveness? ", we must help them to ask such questions and help them to find the answers. Of course, this does not mean that we are to induce a sense of guilt in any child of God. But while a sermon may never provide the personal, deep help that private counseling may give, a sermon may convince an anxious seeker that release from an intolerable inner burden is possible, that there is a blessedness in be-

ing found out, in taking what our fathers called the
way of the cross, the hard and rewarding pathway of
penitence, confession, restitution (when this is possible), and realized forgiveness. In that record of an
age of blood and iron that we know as The Book of
Joshua there is a timeless insight concerning sin and
the necessity of dealing honestly with it. Despite a
clear warning, one of Joshua's company, Achan by
name, had yielded to the temptation of easy money.
He had "'taken some of the devoted things; . . .
stolen, and lied, and put them among their own
stuff.'" "Then Joshua said to Achan, 'My son, give
glory to the Lord God of Israel, and render praise to
him; and tell me now what you have done; do not
hide it from me'" (Josh. 7:19). Achan confessed
and doubtless experienced the release honest confession brings. But primitive religion knew no mercy.
Like confessed political sinners in modern totali-
tarian states, the offender against tribal as well as the
moral law paid with his life. But there is forgiveness
with God not only that he may be feared but that
he may be loved for the love wherewith he forgives
us and gives us another chance. To us has been entrusted the glorious good news that "if we confess
our sins, he is faithful and just, and will forgive our
sins and cleanse us from all unrighteousness."

A few years ago a book appeared to tell its readers
where people take their troubles. As you may sur-
mise, people go to all sorts of places and persons.
Americans and Britishers alike usually try to do something about their difficulties, if only to take an aspirin. If all the pills taken for various deficiencies

and disorders, and many of them efficacious, were
piled in one place, Mt. Everest might have a rival.
A reputable United States journal reported that in a
fourteen-hour daily period, North Americans swal-
low aspirin tablets at an average rate of thirty-three
pounds per minute. I have not verified this appalling
statistic! A little girl asked her grandmother what all
her pills were for. " The yellow pills are for my liver,
the pink ones for my stomach, the black ones are for
my heart, and the green ones are for my nerves." To
which the young grandchild commented, " The red
ones must be to direct traffic." What do people take
for a pain in the conscience, a persistent ache in the
soul caused by sharp and accusing memories? Physi-
cians of the soul do much to ease the distress, al-
though many of them stop short of the complete cure
because they ask:

> " Not, ' Are you saved? ' . . . but an informal,
> Insistent query, ' Brother, are you normal? ' "

Religious people may have overemphasized " sins "
— violations of conventional morality, those devia-
tions from accepted behavior that are more symp-
toms than sin. But it is doubtful if religious people
have overemphasized what the Bible means by sin,
this rebellion against God and separation from God
and his family. Let a person confront God in Christ,
and the response may be that of Peter: " Depart from
me, for I am a sinful man, O Lord." Let a man imagi-
natively stand before the cross, and he will know his
own complicity in the self-centeredness, the pride,
the willful rejection of the best, which crucified the

Lord of life. Thus a sermon on " Forgiveness " may
well follow an outline based on simple, direct questions: " What is forgiveness? " " Do we need it? "
" Where can we find it? " To these questions we have
God's answer. Today, as in all the yesterdays since
Calvary, men and women have taken themselves and
their sins to what John Bunyan called " a place
somewhat ascending " on which stands a cross " and
a little below in the bottom, a sepulcher." Moderns
do not use the language of Bunyan, but his words describe a continuing experience: " So I saw in my
dream that just as Christian came up with the cross,
his burden loosed from off his shoulders, and fell
from off his neck and began to tumble, and so continued to do, till it came to the mouth of the sepulcher, where it fell in, and I saw it no more." In answering these questions as clearly as we can, we
answer the question, Why take ourselves and our deep
trouble to a place in a corner of a vanished empire
where nineteen hundred years ago a young man was
executed for crimes he did not commit? Because there
we confront, and by the miracle of divine grace experience, the action of divine Love.

> " There was no other good enough
>   To pay the price of sin."

Only God can heal this inner wound. For this disease only the divine Physician is able. " It is through
the Son, at the cost of His own blood, that we are
redeemed, freely forgiven through that full and generous grace which has overflowed into our lives and
opened our eyes to the truth " (Eph. 1:7, 8, Phil-

lips). We need a bridgehead toward God, and the gospel proclaims that this has been created. Bridges over vast chasms are usually built from both sides. And the faith claims that God started before man could. He loves us so much that he came personally to this planet to bridge the gulf our sinfulness had made. To change the figure, he focused his love in Jesus Christ, and this focus reaches its burning, healing point in Christ's sacrifice upon the cross " for the sins of the whole world," including yours and mine. We cannot earn it, say the Scriptures. We just accept it. Who was it said, " Faith does not consist in the belief that we are saved; it consists in the belief that we are loved "? While we were yet sinners, God proved, demonstrated, established his love for us in that Christ died for us.

> " I know not how that Calvary's Cross
> A world from sin could free;
> I only know its matchless love
> Has brought God's love to me."

In such preaching of God's remedy for sin we must be as specific as possible in indicating the answer to the final question such preaching may evoke: How do we experience God's forgiveness? Assuredly the answer is the apostle's word to the Philippian jailor: " ' Believe in the Lord Jesus.' " To clarify what " believe " means will help many who think of it chiefly in terms of some intellectual legerdemain, some effort of the will. To show them that it means much more than intellectual assent, more to begin with than consent to a way of life — that it is trust and

obedience — may light the way home for the return-
ing one. You may have found, as I have, that it also
helps inquirers to name some of the rungs on the
ladder of faith down which the Lord comes and up
which his child ascends. An example of this kind of
conclusion to a sermon on " Forgiveness " would in-
clude such directions as:

1. Bring to the surface of your mind every failure, every accusing memory, every hidden shame.
Bring this up decisively.

2. Turn them all over to Christ. When Saint Jerome, scholar of the Early Church, in a dream offered the Lord his books, his research, his good
works, these were declined. He heard the Lord say,
" Jerome, give me your sins that I may pardon
them."

3. Accept Christ's forgiveness. " ' Courage, my
son! ' " said Jesus, " ' your sins are forgiven ' " (Matt.
9:2, Moffatt) .

4. Go forth in that " full and generous grace which
has overflowed " into your life to live the life he has
offered you; a life forgiving, trusting, obedient, and,
within the fellowship of the redeemed, engaged " in
Christ " to seek and to save others who are lost.

> " O dearly, dearly has He loved,
>   And we must love Him, too,
>   And trust in His redeeming blood
>   And try His works to do."

So to preach is to open the channel for God's Spirit
to instill in the soul what the theologian calls " the
courage to accept oneself as accepted in spite of being
unacceptable."

Another sermon or series of Lenten sermons could deal with " Dialogues at the Cross." There was a dialogue at the cross when Jesus of Nazareth died on it. There has been a dialogue ever since.

1. There was a dialogue among the soldiers of the execution squad. It is likely that for some at least it would deal with more than the disposition of his garments (Matt. 27:35) . Soldiers also ask questions, argue, speculate. Is this the way it is? Does love and kindness receive this kind of treatment in a world like this? Is this how unselfish living is rewarded? What's the score? And all the time God was speaking to them in that broken majestic Figure on the central cross. Life is not a jungle or a battlefield. It is more than a market or forum. It is to be life in the family of God, and before you is the Elder Brother and Saviour.

2. The dialogue between sensitive souls confronting the mystery of undeserved suffering. " There were also many women there, looking on from afar, who had followed Jesus from Galilee, ministering to him." Mary of Magdala, and Mary the mother of James and Joseph, and the mother of the sons of Zebedee, and Jesus' mother Mary. And when their sobbing had stopped, the questions would thrust themselves forward. Why does the innocent suffer? Can God be love and permit this? Where is God? And it would not be a one-way conversation. God was speaking to them, and would speak the last word on this injustice and cruelty. The third day would come. Meanwhile, he speaks through his Suffering Servant on Calvary. And as a result one of Christ's later followers would gain the insight that " the pain

God is allowed to guide ends in a saving repentance, never to be regretted, whereas the world's pain ends in death."

3. On Golgotha there was a dialogue between two criminals and Jesus. One of the condemned, twisted by his hatred of society and of himself, railed at the guiltless victim beside him. The other had been moved by this strange encounter with the Man whom he knew to be the victim of judicial murder. The dialogue concerning sin and responsibility and the future proceeds. But to the response the divine mystery seems to make through Christ, the penitent thief makes his own response: " ' Jesus, remember me . . .' " Still through the Man on the cross comes the divine assurance, " ' Today you will be with me in Paradise.' "

4. Most revealing and most awesome in mystery is the dialogue between Jesus and the Father. We hear only one side of it: " ' Father, forgive . . . My God, why . . . ? Father, into thy hands . . .' " What was the response? God himself. And the supreme response, God's final word on the obedience of the Son of his love was Easter.

> ". . . Victory remains with love:
> Jesus, our Lord is crucified! "

And the dialogue proceeds. Now it is between the soul and God. Across the same sharp issues of life and death the conversation continues. Often it seems a conversation at midnight, the midnight of our era, the final hour for man. What is life's meaning? Why do the innocent suffer? How can we be forgiven?

Will God come out victor over every enemy? It is for us to help men to hear God's answer, even while we know that no man can receive it who does not respond with the obedience and service of his life.

> " He is the Truth.
> Seek Him in the Kingdom of Anxiety;
> You will come to a great city
> That has expected your return for years "
> (W. H. Auden, *The Flight Into Egypt*) .

Anxiety like a gray ghost stalks many souls because they have not come to terms with death. If a person is " in Christ," committed to the God who has found him in Jesus Christ, he is delivered from what Browning called man's archfear — the fear of death. A sermon on Christ's offensive against death may well be built around Luke's report of Jesus' interruption of the funeral procession on its way to the cemetery (Luke 7:12–15) . He moves swiftly to the side of the widowed mother bereft of her only son. Divine pity met human grief and banished the bitterness of it. Divine love met human heartbreak and mended it. Divine power met physical death and transformed it. From this Gospel incident, now seen in the light of Christ's resurrection, can we not persuade men and women who are on the way with Christ to go all the way? To accept Christ's offer of life is to live " amid the changes and chances of this mortal life " by the power of an endless life. To confide oneself into the keeping of the divine Love is to experience eternal life here and now and therefore hereafter and forever. When one of Christ's disciples meets the last

LINCOLN BIBLE INSTITUTE

enemy, there is no anxiety or fear. Many will know
of one of the saints of the ecumenical Church, Die-
trich Bonhoeffer, Christian martyr during the clos-
ing weeks of the Nazi regime. This man could have
remained safely in America, where he had done post-
graduate study. He chose to return to Germany, exercise his Christian ministry, and share the trials of
his people. It was not long before his Christian witness involved him in resistance to the Hitler movement. The Gestapo arrested him. An English officer
(Payne Best, in *The Venlo Incident*) who was also a
prisoner in the Flossenbürg prison to which he was
sent paid shining tribute to Bonhoeffer's Christian
witness. " He was one of the very few men that I ever
met to whom his God was real and close to him "
(p. 180). On April 8, 1945, Pastor Bonhoeffer " held
a little service and spoke to us in a manner which
reached the hearts of all, finding just the right words
to express the spirit of our imprisonment and the
thoughts and resolutions which it had brought. He
had hardly finished his last prayer when the door
opened and two evil-looking men in civilian clothes
came in and said: ' Prisoner Bonhoeffer, get ready to
come with us.' Those words ' come with us ' — for
all prisoners that had come to mean one thing only
— the scaffold. We bade him good-by — he drew me
aside — ' This is the end,' he said. ' For me the beginning of life,' and then he gave me a message to
give, if I could, to the bishop of Chichester. . . . Next
day, at Flossenbürg, he was hanged." For every man
and woman " in Christ," let the summons come soon
or late, this should be the meaning of death: " the

beginning of life " in another dimension of existence. Without morbid preoccupation with death, and ever pitching this life high for the Kingdom's sake, Christians come with confidence to the last great adventure. We know whom we have believed. We know also that we must

" Be ready for journey.
The time is prepared for us. What we were is sinking
Under the disposition of what will be.
. . . Now, as the night turns,
A different life, pitched above our experience
Or imagining, is moving about its business.
Tonight — Aaron, Miriam, Shendi — our slavery
Will be gone "

(Christopher Fry, *The First Born*).

V. *"The Human Being Is a Lonely Creature"*

A few years ago one of Scotland's historic houses was offered for sale. According to the August, 1949, number of the United Kingdom Information Office *News from Scotland,* " Castle Gloom " was offered to the public by the present owner. It is located in the little town of Dollar, which was once spelled Dolour or sorrow. All the place names speak of sadness. " Gloom," possibly from the Gaelic *chleum,* was so named until 1490, when the duke of Argyle changed it to Castle Campbell. Here John Knox lived for a time and preached the Reformation. (Let no one suggest that this latter fact explains the designation " Gloom "!) In 1644 the castle was burned and sacked by the Royalist army of Montrose. Had you lived in the fifteenth century and wished to send a letter to a resident of this particular house, you would have addressed it as follows:

" Castle Gloom,
    In the Parish of Dolour (sorrow)
       Beside the water of Grief (now Griff),
      In the Glen of Care."

Many of our fellow citizens have been living there. Christian maturity refuses to be entertained by Giant

Despair in any Castle Gloom, but how many have attained Christian maturity? One poet, Archibald MacLeish (*Atlantic* magazine, July, 1954), found that in his case age brought wisdom:

> " At twenty, stooping round about,
>   I thought the world a miserable place,
>   Truth a trick, faith in doubt,
>   Little beauty, less grace.
>
> " Now at sixty, what I see,
>   Although the world is worse by far,
>   Stops my heart in ecstasy;
>   God, the wonders that there are! "

But many who are sixty, and more who are not, dissent from such joyous reading of the world of nature or of man. Consider this passage written over one hundred years ago (September, 1849) by Matthew Arnold to Arthur Hugh Clough:

> " These are damned times. Everything is against one — the height to which our knowledge is come, the spread of luxury, our physical enervation, the absence of great natures, the unavoidable contact with millions of little ones; newspapers, cities, light, profligate friends, moral desperadoes like Carlyle, our own selves and the sickening consciousness of our difficulties."

Except for Carlyle, and possibly the " light, profligate friends," this catalogue of woes is up to date. We know what Arnold meant by " the sickening con-

sciousness of our difficulties." Powerful, unpredict-
able enemies abroad; an intense struggle for power
between East and West; a weakening of confidence
in our own way of life tempting its frightened sup-
porters to use enemy tactics to defeat the enemy; in-
sidious spread of fear, suspicion, and hatred among
allies; the high cost of living and dying in an atomic
age — we know what it is to be lonely, discouraged.
To plague us also there remains Arnold's other cause
of despair: " our own selves." No one needs to be a
Neo-orthodox theologian to realize the " fallenness "
about us. Dr. Raymond B. Fosdick, until recently di-
rector of the Rockefeller Foundation, surveyed our
world and its plight and reached this conclusion:

> " What has been bombed out and dissipated
> is not primarily a smoothly running system
> for the production of consumable goods, but
> rather *hope* and *faith* and the belief that the
> individual, in all his magnificence and mis-
> ery, is the final criterion of worth."

Any way you look — to use the speech of the man in
the street — it's grim, rugged, tough. Any way but
one way — the way of the wandering star that marked
the birthplace of a Child, the way of a cross on which
a Man died, the way of an open tomb hard by the
cross, the way of an upper room and a Presence
transforming a little group of utterly depressed men
into " the Holy Catholic Church."
But it is simply untrue to say that a majority of
men and women in our so-called Christian countries
look that way or take *the* Way. As Dr. John Baillie

observed, there are more hopeless people today than there are people who cherish false and illusory hopes. Here is where we come in; or, rather, here is where the Holy Spirit comes in, using us to convey the living hope. To the inhabitants of a global Castle Gloom we bring great news. It is the news enshrined in the Biblical view of life. To the question, " Who is winning? — God or the devil, Christ or Antichrist, life or death " — we have the answer. In the advent, life, teaching, death, and resurrection of the Lord Jesus Christ the crisis of history has been reached and the essential victory won. As New Testament scholars such as Dr. Oscar Cullman have phrased it, we live " in the interval between the decisive battle and Victory Day." As the New Testament jubilantly affirms: " We have been born anew to a living hope through the resurrection of Jesus Christ from the dead." This note of unquenchable hope is struck again and again in our Scriptures: " ' The hour is coming, indeed it has come,' " " The light shines in the darkness, and the darkness has not overcome it." " As it is, we do not yet see everything in subjection to him. But we see Jesus . . . crowned with glory and honor." What is this hope? Paul set it down memorably in his letter to the Christian colony in Rome: " The hope being that creation as well as man would one day be freed from its thraldom to decay and gain the glorious freedom of God's children. . . . We were saved with this hope ahead " (Rom. 8:21, 24 Moffatt) .

Such hope is not of our making, nor can we hang it in our sky as we place a tinsel star on a Christmas

tree. This hope, like faith and love, is God's gift.
Concerning faith we may say " have faith," " believe." Concerning love, someone may command,
" Thou shalt love." But hope in the New Testament
sense is that for which we quietly wait. It comes to
him who waits — in the right place; and the right
place is where God meets us in Christ Jesus. With
this hope in us we purify ourselves as he is pure, not
only disinfecting ourselves of the sins which so easily
drag us down, but of the despair about ourselves, our
fellow souls, and the world God loved and loves. In
December, 1954, the French premier, M. Mendes-
France, announced that he had appointed a former
French airman to be secretary of state for youth. This
cabinet member, said the prime minister, would be
in charge of hope, would instill courage and high ex-
pectancy in the youth of France from sixteen years
of age to sixty-five. In a sense we have been called to
a similar ministry, for we are entrusted with the hope
that is in Christ. Unlike the heroine of the musical
play *South Pacific,* many of our people are not
" stuck like a dope with a thing called hope "; they
are stuck in a morass of hopelessness. To them we
must put the psalmist's question, " Why are you cast
down . . . why are you disquieted within? " (Ps.
42:11) and help them to answer. Of course, we shall
give the Biblical prescription: " Hope in God," but
such a true but vague direction is of little help to
religiously illiterate folk. Therefore, the preacher
makes clear what the faith means by God, remem-
bering always that he is infinitely greater than anything the wisest minds can say about him. (1) To

hope in God, to believe in the God of the Christian
revelation, is to confide ourselves and our world into
the keeping of the great God who created the universe
and who is still creating it. From stars to atoms he
is engaged in perfecting that which concerns him.
" ' My Father is working still,' " said the Son who
knew him best. This infinite creative Spirit is also
fatherly. " As a father pities His children, so the
Lord. . . . He remembers that we are dust," and
also his children.

> " Fatherlike, He tends and spares us;
> Well our feeble frame He knows."

(2) The great and gracious God is also the redeemer
of the world he has made and is making. Infinite
wisdom, power, love, has " visited and redeemed his
people " in the person and action of a man like ourselves, Jesus Christ. Before his death, H. G. Wells
finally despaired of man, was sure that the universe
had become bored with its most troublesome deni-
zen. " Mankind," he concluded bitterly, " which began in a cave and behind a windbreak, will end in
a disease-soaked ruins of a slum " (*The Fate of Homo
Sapiens*). Thinkers outside the faith who have found
the illusory hopes of secular optimism untenable are
tempted to agree. But the hope that is born of the experience of God's saving love is sure that man is
something more than " the biologic smear on Planet
No. 3." It lifts up its tremendous song: " Beloved,
we are God's children now; it does not yet appear
what we shall be, but we know that when he appears
we shall be like him, for we shall see him as he is."

In an early poem, "Birches," one of America's best-loved poets, Robert Frost, expresses a common desire:

> "I'd like to get away from earth awhile
> And then come back to it and begin over."

God knew we should feel like that and need that kind of flight, not from reality, but to the reality that can fill us with all joy and peace in believing. So on the wings of faith we rise to the summit of that hill on which incarnate Love suffered and died that we might be forgiven, accepted, infused with newness of life, and thus abound in hope. From that place, so truly "out of this world" and yet within this world of sin and splendor, we come "back and begin over." To trust this God who confronts us in the crucified and risen Saviour is to know that we are loved creatures, cannot be utterly worthless, and can be forgiven all but our despair. (3) Christian faith and experience point to one other tremendous fact concerning the God of hope. Infinite Spirit that God is, he is not remote or inaccessible in this illimitable universe, nor merely to be known as active back in history. Hope thou in God, the Lord and Giver of life. He is the life within our lives, "than self more near." He is the Paraclete, the One who stands beside, the Guide and Companion and Counselor within. "I believe in the Holy Ghost." John Steinbeck the novelist not only does skillful scavenging but surprisingly lyrical preaching in his writing. In *East of Eden* he utters his credo. With blunt candor he acknowledges the forces which in the name of the group "have declared a war on that preciousness, the mind of man. . . . By disparagement, by starvation, forced direction, and the stunning hammer blows of conditioning, the free, roving mind is being pursued, roped, blunted, drugged." Yet in face of such demonic assaults on the citadel of man's intellectual and spiritual life, the novelist avows his faith: " This I believe: that the free, exploring mind of the individual human is the most valuable thing in the world." Why? Because every " individual human " is " the temple of the Holy Spirit," because of the tremendous value placed by God on the most insignificant member of his human family. So can the Christian minister " in charge of hope " send previously dispirited men and women forth, not into a glen of gloom, but into a vale of soul-making with One who makes any terrain a field of honor. It was said of Robert Louis Stevenson's father that he always considered life " a shambling sort of omnibus taking him to his hotel." Well, life is no omnibus, but a stiff climb uphill most of the way. Thank God, there is the staff of faith to support us, the best of companions with whom to journey, and a Presence to guide and sustain to journey's end and beyond. Hence to everyman we say in Christ's stead, Put your confidence in the triune God. Make but trial of his love, and you will yet praise him who is our help and our God.

As Christian preachers, are we then to assume that those who are without hope because without God in their world view are exercised about it? That when a world council or a parish minister announces a message on hope all will be interested? Who that knows the apathy, the unwillingness to face reality, the absorption in trivia which characterize so many of God's children would assume so much? Two weeks before his death in 1946, Logan Pearsall Smith, the expatriated American man of letters, was asked by a friend, half jokingly, if he had discovered any meaning in life. " Yes," he replied, " there is a meaning; at least for me, there is one thing that matters — to set a chime of words tinkling in the minds of a few fastidious people." " And the state, Logan," the friend went on, " the family, the international situation, Russia, India? " Propped up on his pillows, he waved all this away with his hand. " A chime of words," he repeated, " a few discriminating people " (Cyril Connolly, *Ideas and Places*). One might expect such blithe repudiation of living issues in a dilettante aged eighty-one. One suspects that many younger persons who could not care less for a chime of words and are not enamored of fastidious people have as little concern about the important issues of life and death.

" Do you think the world will end with a bang or a
    whimper?
    I'm rather inclined to think it won't end with a
    bang —
More probably with a simper,
    Like that on the face of the little orangoutang
In Bronx Park when he's feeling so pleased with
    himself "

             (John Hall Wheelock,
   Random Reflections on a Cloudless Sunday) .

Yet we must not be deceived by the façade of con-
tentment behind which contemporaries live or the
absorption in the ephemeral by which they avoid
tangling with great matters. If we could penetrate
the disguises, we should understand why modern
man has never been the same since the childlike faith
and starry hopes died.

> " Not that he says much, but he laughs
>   Much louder than he used to.
>   And he can't bear to be left alone even for
>   a minute, and he can't
>   Sit still.
>   . . . Man was ever so much happier before
>   His Father died."

Miss Edna St. Vincent Millay, in reporting " Conversation at Midnight," added this revealing line
about man in the second half of this century of progress:

" He gets along pretty well as long as it's daylight."

But the night comes — and then? In the King James
Version of the Song of Solomon (ch. 3:8) there is a
vivid phrase which we can " re-mythologize " to describe non-Christian society: " Every man hath his
sword . . . [beside him] because of fear in the
night " (R.S.V.: " against alarms by night "). After
prolonged study of the North American scene, Cyril
Connolly thought about the American way of life.
He concluded that it is " one of the most effective
the world has ever known, but about the end of life
Americans are more in the dark than any people

since the Gauls of Tacitus. . . . It may be summed
up as a creed which is partly the effect of climate,
partly of vitamins and calories, partly of pioneer ex-
periences, partly of the inherited memory of what
was bad in Europe. The American way assumes a
world without God, yet a world in which happiness
is obtainable. . . . But the end? What is old age in
America? After sixty where do old people vanish?
Why are the bustling battalions of unwanted Moms
so elegantly pathetic? And the rich who have pock-
eted their winnings, why are they so glum? And what
is this ' way,' in reality, but forty years of drudgery
in an office while the divorced wives play bridge together and the children drift apart? What is the
getting of money but a constant source of ulcers
and anxiety, till apoplexy or heart failure clamps
down? . . . And why the immense rush to psychia-
try, the high rate of madness and suicide? Why, after
midnight, do so many Americans fight or weep? "
(Cyril Connolly, *Ideas and Places*). America is not
all so black, nor are all Americans so destitute of
sense. Nevertheless Mr. Connolly has perceived truly
that in the world's most prosperous nation man without God or hope " gets along pretty well as long as
it's daylight." Acts, ch. 16, tells of another conversation at midnight. Two Christian leaders, thrown into
jail because of the effects of their " subversive " activity, start a commotion by " praying and singing
hymns to God." This unusual service of witness
ended in a completely successful evangelistic mission
to the jailer and his household. " What of us? "
Christopher Fry has the people of South England ask

Cuthman, Saint of Sussex, at the conclusion of his play *The Boy with a Cart:*

" What of us who have to catch up, always
   To catch up with the high-powered car, or with
   The unbalanced budget, to cope with competition,
   To weather the sudden thunder of the uneasy
   Frontier? We also loom with the earth
   Over the waterways of space. Between
   Our birth and death we may touch understanding
   As a moth brushes a window with its wings."

But no such contact with understanding, no discernment of life's meaning and hope, no knowledge of " more than the gossip that comes to us over our gates," will be made unless the Word from beyond comes through.

Does the Word ever come through such faulty instruments as ourselves unless we know and speak intelligibly to the deep needs of those who may hear us? One of these needs is for reassurance that what should be shall be, that to Christ and not to Caesar belongs the future. " Who's winning? " is a good question on which to make a sermon. Together the preacher and his people look at the chief answers, that of secular despair, the answer of secular and religious optimism, and finally the answer of Christian " belief-full realism." In the midst of social turbulence, the Christian yields neither to hysteria nor to complacency but exhibits what Reinhold Niebuhr calls " genuine Christian nonchalance." Why? Because with the eyes of faith he sees in the faithfulness of Christians, in their witness and service of Christ, preview of the final score. Like his Lord during the mission of the Seventy, the believer sees in the fidelity of today's disciples the doom of evil. " ' I saw Satan fall like lightning from heaven . . . rejoice that your names are written in heaven ' " (Luke 10:17, 20). " Where is your carpenter now? " asked a Roman of a Christian, as both watched the martyrdom of other Christians in the arena. Back came the answer, " Making a coffin for your emperor."

Reassurance as to the final score in the unending conflict is but one need of the human being we would reach with the good news. One of the profound needs of the personality is for friendship, for life in true community. Therefore, one of the deadly enemies of spiritual health and effectiveness is loneliness. Doubtless part of the price to be paid for being human is a sense of loneliness which overtakes the best adjusted person.

> " Praise to harmony, to love.
> They are best, all else is false.
> Yet even in love and harmony
> The human being is a lonely creature "
>   (Richard Eberhart).

For several years a former minister of City Temple, London, the late Dr. Joseph Fort Newton, conducted a syndicated newspaper column in many North American newspapers. As a result, he received an immense number of letters, most of them asking for help on vexatious problems. Dr. Newton classified the questions and found that the chief topics of

his correspondence were four, which he described as
the private enemies of people. Pressing fear and anxiety for first place was loneliness. In a scholarly study
of the individual isolated in modern society (Mar-
garet Mary Wood, *Paths of Loneliness*) , the author
agreed that the accent in modern society is on alone-
ness; that many of us feel alone, unrelated to others,
unable to feel at one with those about us. She asked,
" Why is it that in a world in which modern transportation and communication have brought us face
to face with our fellows throughout the world we
should often feel emotionally and spiritually alone? "
Who has not asked such questions? A growing litera-
ture on the problem helps us to understand " the nature of the sundering powers." Three significant
books, Erich Fromm's *Escape from Freedom,* David
Riesman's *The Lonely Crowd,* and Paul Halmos'
Solitude and Privacy, contribute insights. Freed from
the bonds of a simpler, more cohesive, society, in
which he had a real sense of belonging to the group,
modern man is more of an individual than ever. As
a result, he is more alone and anxious in a world in
which he is unable to establish emotionally satisfying
social relationships. So Erich Fromm's thesis. As for
North Americans who are middle-class, urban citizens, David Riesman finds that most of these never
really come close to others or to themselves. Western
man is so anxious for the approval of others in his
group that he is a conformist fearful of being re-
garded by other conformists as eccentric, different,
" radical." The third inquiry seems to follow a similar line, emphasizing man's biological need to be

" other-directed." Man's loneliness and related problems arise from the frustration of his " biosocial
needs," — which I understand to mean that man is
lonely often because in our society he has fewer and
fewer opportunities for spontaneous, unreserved social participation.

Any Christian will perceive that conformity as a
means to escape loneliness is fraught with spiritual
danger. In the sarcastic idiom of today, How well-
adjusted can Christians get? A sermon on this theme,
using the ever popular story of the " three Hebrew
children " (Dan. 3:17, 18) and Rom. 12:2, will rally
flagging loyalties today as it did when it was written
to inspirit the harassed Jews of the second century
before Christ who were being persecuted into conformity by Antiochus Epiphanes. Self-adjustment is
one of Christianity's specialities. But self-adjustment
is not the complete goal of the Christian life, any
more than to attain " a tranquil sense of effortless su-
periority " is man's chief end. Christians rightly seek
to be as well adjusted as their Lord. But such adjustment never means supine acceptance of things as they
are when things as they are deprive anyone anywhere
of the chance to live the good, the abundant, the
Christlike life. " Have you found peace, my brother? "
asked a well-intentioned but misguided evangelist of
William Wilberforce when the latter was on his way
home from the defeat of one of his reform measures
in the House of Commons. " No," snapped the re-
former, " I have found war." " ' I have not come to
bring peace, but a sword,' " said the Prince of Peace.

As for sermons directed to the inner needs of

lonely and anxious persons, the sentimental and superficial treatment given in much " pulpit counseling " should not deter us from preaching to such conditions with as much of the gospel as we can bring. A series of sermons, particularly if a second Sunday service is available, on everyday questions may bring persons to inquire in the temple: " Are You Lonely? " (Luke 19:5, 6: " And when Jesus came to the place, he looked up and said to him, ' Zacchaeus, make haste and come down; for I must stay at your house today.' So he made haste and came down, and received him joyfully.") A kind of imaginative " case study " of Zacchaeus and his isolation, linked with Christ's cure, might prove singularly therapeutic for someone who feels homesick in his home and condemned to lay his head " in a foreign land, whenever the day is done." More wonderful and therefore more difficult of exposition is the saying of our Lord recorded in the Fourth Gospel: " ' Alone . . . yet I am not alone, for the Father is with me ' " (John 16:32).

" Are You in the Right Place? " is another question which will appeal to more " settled " persons than we imagine. It sounds like the kind of query asked by a vocational guidance expert, or a traffic policeman. James Agate has an illuminating entry in *The Later Ego:* " For the man of richly stored mind, any place is the right place." Do we agree? What about a richly stored soul? a heart " hid with Christ in God "? Philippians 4:11–13 is the textual passage that seems indicated.

" Are You Afraid of the Future? " brings the af-

firmation of I Cor. 3:21–23 into the focal center of
attention: " All things are yours . . . the future, all
are yours; and you are Christ's; and Christ is God's."
However simply we restate our Christian confidence
that the tomorrows belong to God, one soul may re-
solve gallantly to commit the future to his care, persuaded that invincible love lives, works, reigns.

" Has Someone Hurt You? " may seem to be a de-
liberate invitation to wallow in self-pity. Yet in a sermon seeking to deal with the problem of injustice, of
unkindness, God's Word may come with power to
cleanse and heal. It does seem that most of us respond to injuries either in the spirit of the writer of
Ps. 109, which Sir George Adam Smith described as
" the delirium of the conscience produced by a fam-
ine of justice " (see Moffatt), or with the mind of
our Lord expressed in Matt. 5:43–45. One man
found his sermon plan following simple, obvious
" directives ":

1. Consider the high cost of hating. (If 60 per
cent of all disease has an emotional origin, many of
the maladies must be caused by resentment and
anger.) 2. Face the resentment as objectively as you
can. 3. As you face the resentment, try to discover
if the cause is valid. It may be due to your own hy-
persensitiveness or to misunderstanding of another's
motives. 4. Take the way of Christ. Is it casuistry to
say that " Christians are people who love people
whom they do not like "? To take Christ's way is to
move up from the legal level to that of love. This
means that Christ must dwell in our hearts by faith,
that the love of Christ may express itself in prayer

and blessing of the " enemy " who curses us. It means
further that we employ a secret strategy of the saints:
we try to do some positive good to the person whom
we have resented. Finally, to have this mind in us
which was also in Christ Jesus requires us never to
turn back again and reopen the old wound. Following an act of genuine forgiveness, we are to put the
injury behind our back as God does.

" Let nothing linger after, no whimpering ghost re-
    main
  In wall or beam or rafter, or any hate or pain.
  Cleanse and call home thy spirit."

  " Do you feel insignificant? " may be a springboard
to dive into deeper waters than the gospel of self-help
commonly floats in. " As servants of God we com-
mend ourselves in every way . . . as unknown, and
yet well known " (II Cor. 6:4, 9). It may hearten one
of life's " nobodies " to remind him how richly significant have been the parts played by the so-called
anonymous. Also that whether known or unknown
we may experience what another called the most satisfying happiness known to man: the joy of self-
expression in work well done, for God's sake and the
sake of others. Moving into the center of the faith,
the preacher points to One who made himself of no
reputation, carried his obedience to God's will " even
to die, and to die upon the cross " (Phil. 2:5-9,
Moffatt). Finally, we are to find our reward not in
recognition by others but in the approval of Him
whom having not seen we love. After the apostle
cites the axiom of responsible citizenship in God's

Kingdom (I Cor. 4:2–4), " It is required of stewards that they be found trustworthy," he goes on to say, " But with me it is a very small thing that I should be judged by you or by any human court. I do not even judge myself. . . . It is the Lord who judges me." " Gentlemen, in every audience," said Edwin Booth, the once eminent Shakespearean actor, " there is a king. Play to the king."

" Do You Want Security? " seems like a silly question to ask in the era of the welfare state. But there is a kind of spiritual security that many crave and cannot find in a social security card. Luke 12:13–31, the story of the Rich Fool, is an obvious Scriptural basis for a sermon in which others may be helped to realize that when we ask for absolute security in this kind of world we ask for too much; that God gives the grace of insecurity that we may find our stability and safety in him alone.

" Are You Frustrated? " recalls one of the animated cartoon characters of that unusual artist Walter Disney. But it is no laughing matter when so much of life's tragedy comes from thwarted hopes, broken dreams, unfulfilled aspirations. More than Moses on Mount Nebo hear life or God saying, " ' I have let you see it with your eyes, but you shall not go over there ' " (Deut. 34:4). How does Christ help us make frustrations fruitful? Is it not true that one door is closed in order that another may be opened? that to block our progress on a chosen road may prove ultimately to be a blessing? Paul's experience with his thorn in the flesh, the blocked plans, the " many adversaries," and the " wide door for effective work "

may light lamps for discouraged pilgrims in this year
of grace.

"How Can I Handle Trouble?" sends minister
and people alike to two passages: 1. Gen. 42:36 —
Jacob's complaint: "'You have bereaved me of my
children: Joseph is no more, and Simeon is no more,
and now you would take Benjamin; all this has come
upon me,'" (The King James Version is even more
striking: "All these things are against me.")

2. Rom. 5:3, 4: "But we triumph even in our troubles" (Moffatt). An alternative passage, of course,
would be Phil. 1:12–14: "I want you to know, brethren, that what has happened to me has really served
to advance the gospel . . ."

A question often heard in households when Junior
is invisible has overtones of deep spiritual meaning:
"Where Are You?" "The Lord God called to the
man, and said to him, 'Where are you?'" (Gen.
3:9). Where are we in relation to the significant
movements of life? Where are we in our relationships
to persons? And, since the question was asked by
God: Where are we in relation to him? Have we
moved from the I-Thou or I-It to Thou-I? If you
know Thornton Wilder's homespun play *Our Town,*
you will remember the answer given to a girl by one
who wrote this as her complete mailing address:

> "Jane Crofut,
>   The Crofut Farm,
>   Grover's Corners,
>   Sutton County,
>   New Hampshire,
>   United States of America,

> "Continent of North America,
>   Western Hemisphere,
>   The Earth,
>   The Solar System,
>   The Universe,
>   The Mind of God."

No one is ever at home who is without such an ultimate cosmic reference. To be a spiritual vagrant with no fixed abode is to be, of all pilgrims, the most miserable. Thus we cannot leave this question, or ones like it such as "Who do you think you are?", without leaving our hearts and ourselves in the presence of Him who is our eternal home, as well as "our Help in ages past, our Hope for years to come."

Entrusted with the good news of God as we are, and seeking always to proclaim it with relevance, interest, and meaning, do we ever reach our objective unless our hearers confront Christ face to face? A college historian (Lynn White, Jr., "The Changing Past," *Harper's* magazine, November, 1954, p. 33) points out that in the later twelfth and thirteenth centuries "a seismic shift began to take place in the nature of Christian piety." This was revealed unconsciously in religious art. "A conservative Spanish bishop, Luke of Tuy, sensed what was happening: he denounced pictures of 'one-eyed Virgins,' by which he meant representations of Saint Mary in profile. His fears were well grounded." Up to that time Christian art had been largely frontal, as that of the Eastern Church still is. Such pictures and images "establish a direct and almost hypnotic relationship

with the worshiper, whom they fix with their eyes:
they form an art capable of conveying power and
spiritual grace. But as soon as the eyes of the image
shift from the worshiper, religious art becomes drama
rather than sacrament, and the worshiper tends to
become merely a spectator." For example, early pictures of the Last Supper show Christ taking the bread
and saying, " This is my body which is broken for
you." The emphasis is sacramental. But the new way
showed the sop being given to Judas. The bread of
salvation did not seem to the late medieval mind as
significant as the moment of Judas' condemnation.
Increasingly this is the case until, as the historian
phrases it, " the human situation has displaced the
transit of divine grace as the center of attention."
Similarly, pictures of the Virgin, which earlier
showed her startled by the intrusion of the archangel
Gabriel with his message, are succeeded by pictures
of Mary at prayer or reading Holy Writ. Listen to
this summary of the change, and ask if it does not
apply to much of Protestant preaching: " In other
words, in early Christianity, when God speaks man
hears. In the later period the mind must be prepared
for the divine message. The focus of religion shifts
away from the saving power which comes from outside man and centers on the problem of human adjustment. For the last seven centuries, this tendency,
despite periodic reactions, has continued. In our own
time Christian Science, psychosomatic medicine, and
psychoanalysis have made, not merely salvation (re-
named ' adjustment ') , but physical health itself, de-
pendent upon the subjective psychological state of

the individual. From his standpoint, Bishop Luke of Tuy was entirely correct."

To confront men with Christ is to bring them where God comes to meet them " head on." It is to lead them to that " collision " with Reality through which God speaks most clearly, most personally, most decisively. So to meet him and to hear him makes life forever different.

Shortly before his death during World War II, Stephen Vincent Benét published a modern miracle play in verse, *A Child Is Born*. He describes what might have happened at the Bethlehem inn the night Christ was born. The characters symbolize ourselves. In the last scene the innkeeper, his wife, and their friends tell each other why they did not visit the stable behind the inn to see the child. As each reproaches himself for his failure to do what Wise Men and shepherds had wisdom and goodness to do, the innkeeper's wife reflects on what has happened. In her soliloquy she says:

" God pity us indeed, for we are human,
    And do not always see
    The vision when it comes, the shining change,
    Or, if we see it, do not follow it
    Because it is too hard, too strange, too new,
    Too unbelievable, too difficult,
    Warring too much with common easy ways. . . .

" Life is not lost by dying! Life is lost
    Minute by minute, day by dragging day,
    In all the thousand small, uncaring ways,

The smooth appeasing compromises of time,
Which are King Herod and King Herod's men.

" Always and always, Life can be
Lost without vision, but not lost by death,
Lost by not caring, willing, going on
Beyond the ragged edge of fortitude
To something more — something no man has seen.
You who love money, you who love yourself,
You who love bitterness, . . .
And all the people of this little town,
Rise up! The loves we had were not enough.
Something is loosed to change the shaken world,
And with it we must change."

My brothers in Christ, God himself has entrusted us with his glorious good news that we may speak that Word. Those who receive it — receive him — acknowledge that

". . . The loves we had were not enough.
Something is loosed to change the shaken world,
And with it we must change."

251
M16e

Date Due

FEB 19 '87			
F			

LINCOLN BIBLE INSTITUTE
PRINTED IN U. S. A.